Praise for *Workplace Stability*

"Real-life examples of the impact of poverty in the U.S. workplace. If we stabilize our workforce, we will have stronger companies with revenue for expansion—a win-win for everyone."

–Judy Byrnes, Former District Manager, Sears Commercial

"It's realistic, avoids controversial workplace/employer flashpoints, and handles the employer's point of view elegantly while balancing the needs of the employee and employer."

–Philip DeVol, Author, *Getting Ahead in the Workplace*

"I am very excited about the release of this book! As a Bridges certified trainer who sits on the workforce development committee, we need this for our community! We have companies with lines shut down because they do not have a healthy workforce."

–Carol Steegman, Bridges Coordinator, Hope House

"Specifically written for employers and extremely helpful for anyone concerned about ROI and employee retention."

–Gilda Shelby, Job Placement and Retention Specialist, HopeWorks

"This book is a valuable addition to the literature for executives and managers who aspire to create an engaged and productive workforce. As a former executive at a nonprofit with a diverse staff, I would have welcomed the insights and guidance Weirich shares here."

–Yvonne Forman, Former Executive Director,
PAX – Program of Academic Exchange

"With Workplace Stability *I realized many successful managers are fortunate to come from stable environments but overlook the impact of unstable environments on employees. This book helps create a foundation of stability not only for employees but for organizations as well."*

–Kevin McKiernan, Director of Strategic Relationships,
MBS Textbook Exchange

Workplace
STABILITY

Creating conditions
that lead to retention,
productivity, and
engagement in
entry-level workers

Weirich, Ruth K.
    Workplace Stability: Creating conditions that lead to retention,
    productivity, and engagement in entry-level workers.
    152 pp.
    Bibliography pp. 133–138

ISBN: 978-1-938248-75-7

Copy editing by Jesse Conrad
Book design by Paula Nicolella
Cover design by Amy Alick Perich

Workplace
STABILITY

Creating conditions
that lead to retention,
productivity, and
engagement in
entry-level workers

Ruth K. Weirich

TABLE OF CONTENTS

ACKNOWLEDGMENTS

The businesses, communities, and individuals who have used aha! Process's work on economic class before me have been my mentors and trainers. Many a business across the United States has done pioneering work with the strategies of Bridges Out of Poverty, and the low-wage and entry-level employees who experience daily instability have taught me so much about that environment—and about how meaningful employer support is.

I've learned so much from Ruby Payne, author of *A Framework for Understanding Poverty* and coauthor of *Bridges Out of Poverty,* as she was the first educator to bring economic class and its effects on individuals and communities to the forefront of the national discussion.

Thank you to Philip DeVol, coauthor of *Bridges Out of Poverty* and author of *Getting Ahead in a Just-Gettin'-By World,* for his thinking about poverty and community sustainability. His wisdom and zen make him a treat to work with.

Thank you to Debra Whitehead and Beth Kuhn, who contributed to the project early on by creating the first outlines for aha! Process's work in the business sector.

A big thank you to all of the people from whom I've learned. Thank you to the following people for granting me time to interview you for this book: Sonia Holycross, Carol Steegman, Amber Werner, Michelle Wood, Ermina Soler, Marvin Green, Mary Hicks, LeLinda Ingram, Nyekiesha Marshall, Jamie Kearney, Jesse Quintana, Renee Salazar, Angela Steinbrecher, Susan Chrisman, Dave Barrett, Beth Pace, Lori DuFour,

Sharon Berry, Shannen Millard, Victoria Sidener, Jane Canale, Nicole Baptiste, Nathan Mandsager, James Vander Hulst, James Connolly, Chad Tuttle, Joyce Gutierrez-Marsh, and Fred Keller. I learned from each of you, and your stories and comments have enriched this book for each reader.

Who can write a book without a quality editor and publications team? Thank you, Peggy Conrad, for your sound guidance and always patient spirit. Thank you to Paula Nicolella for your design expertise, and a big thank you to Jesse Conrad for your attention to detail.

Ultimately this process was made easier because of my husband, Scott Weirich. Because he picked up the slack, I was able to spend the countless hours that working on the book and workshop required. Thank you, thank you.

INTRODUCTION

The behaviors, habits, and patterns of low-wage and entry-level employees often leave business owners and managers scratching their heads. An employee might be fired from a position only to return three days later asking when the boss would "stop being mad" and hire them back. Perhaps an employee suddenly stopped coming to work or started arriving late every day. Maybe an employer promoted an employee from within but was confused by that person's behavior after the promotion. Or maybe an employee surprised management by turning down a promotion. Situations like these can lead some employers to think their low-wage workers are lazy, "takers," and unreliable.

This book is for businesspeople who are tired of the turnover treadmill, absenteeism, lack of productivity, motivation issues, language barriers, and disciplinary problems experienced with some entry-level, lower-wage employees. This book will explore how employees' economic class affects the success of the business. The economic environment people grew up in plays a large part in how they view the world, the work environment, and their personal relationships. Understanding these effects is crucial to working effectively with lower-wage employees whose day-to-day environments are unstable.

Employees living in daily instability face obstacles that are virtually unknown to people living in daily stability. If you live in daily instability, you often operate from a scarcity mentality—you have "less than you feel you need."[1] This mentality does not allow people to plan for the future, a key factor in operating a business. People whose daily lives are unstable are great problem solvers, reactively solving what each day throws at them. But the focus on daily necessities leaves little time to plan for the future. A goal of this book is to help employers better understand low-wage employees. As employers clear up misconceptions and align business and employee needs, they create a dynamic, flexible environment with work accommodations that benefit the business and the employee both.

The world of work operates according to expectations and norms shaped by an environment that is stable on a daily basis. Just as businesspeople sometimes find the norms and expectations of people from daily instability foreign and confusing, low-wage employees who have been living in daily instability for multiple generations walk into a work environment that is foreign to them. This book will explore the various reasons employees living in poverty have a different take on work than human resources personnel, managers, and executives.

The core concepts in this book come from the published works of the consulting company aha! Process and its research on poverty, which has proven its effectiveness in many sectors in the last 20 years. The first business to use *A Framework for Understanding Poverty* by Ruby Payne[2] was Cascade Engineering in Grand Rapids, Michigan. Above all, Cascade CEO Fred Keller wanted to figure out how to have a business answering the needs of all employees as opposed to being very selective of some employees such as mid-level management and executives. At the same time, Cascade was experiencing a 60% turnover rate among all employees. In a nutshell, the management team did not understand the environment of daily instability and the chaos it was causing the business. Employees in Cascade's new welfare-to-career program did not understand the middle class expectations of the workplace.

Cascade came across Payne's book while looking for ways to improve their program. Ten years later Cascade had nearly perfected the program, and employee turnover was down to just 5%.

Keller outlines three things that made the program a success:

- The first step was creating an accepting corporate culture. They had a paradigm shift about how they were going to do business to get the results they wanted. Leadership recognized a disconnect between the culture of their organization and the unstable environment of poverty. They identified obstacles caused by daily instability that were creating pains for the business and the employees alike.

- The second step was training new and existing employees on economic class diversity. This created an awareness of potential issues among all employees, new and old, management and entry level, and gave them a shared vocabulary to address those issues if they arose.

- Cascade's final step was to develop a network of support for employees who were moving from daily instability to daily stability. This included partnering with local government and charitable organizations to provide caseworkers and retention specialists on site. This kept the employees at work while addressing their life issues and headed off employee conflicts before termination was necessary; often the conflict was caused by the obstacles of daily instability.[3]

Dave Barrett, director of talent management at Cascade, says that before they integrated aha! Process principles, their 60% employee turnover rate among all employees cost them $3.6 million per year. With that rate reduced to less than 5%, turnover costs them less than $500,000.

The book *Bridges Out of Poverty* was released by the publishing company aha! Process in 1999[4] and was written for nonprofit agencies serving individuals in poverty. Bridges is a book, movement, and set of strategies that addresses poverty from an economic class perspective. The book focuses on how to work more effectively with clients living in poverty by building better understanding of the environment in which they live. Not only can understanding the environments of daily instability, stability, and long-term stability allow organizations to work more effectively with their clients at the individual level, it creates opportunities to effect change in the organization and the community at the policy level. Policy changes at that level provide stability to individuals and save money for the community. Bridges has grown into a global movement involving communities and organizations in the United States, Canada, Australia, the Czech Republic, Scotland, Mexico, and Slovakia.

Vectren is a utility company in Evansville, Indiana, that uses information from *Framework* and *Bridges Out of Poverty*[5] to educate its call center employees. These employees work directly with households having difficulties paying their monthly utility bills. Beth Pace, a customer outreach representative at Vectren,[6] told me this training has created an awareness and sensitivity to the client base that allows them to work more effectively with their customers.

In addition to Cascade and Vectren, there are a range of business examples—from a frozen food distributor to healthcare providers, from manufacturers to restaurant owners and fast food franchisees—all using concepts from *Framework* and *Bridges* to stabilize the workforce, retain employees, improve productivity, and increase profits. I will share their stories throughout the book.

Bridges Out of Poverty coauthor Phil DeVol has also developed curricula for use with people living in daily instability through a 16-session process in which they investigate instability and stability on their own terms. These Getting Ahead books[7] and workshops are designed for people working to stabilize their daily lives by building resources. The 16-session Getting Ahead in the Workplace model encourages employees to investigate their resources, see the need for change, and decide for themselves what they will do to make their lives more stable.

Because no one likes to be told they must change, the Getting Ahead co-investigative process of discovery results in lasting changes made by intrinsically motivated participants. If the doctor simply tells a patient to lose 15 pounds now, that person probably won't lose the weight because the patient didn't make that decision autonomously. Those pounds will never drop off. But if the doctor shows the patient the need for change by helping the patient understand the costs and benefits, that person will make the same choice with intrinsic motivation—and the patient will see it through because the decision was theirs. This book details many positive impacts Getting Ahead has had on employees: achieving promotions from within, recognizing the value of formal language, respecting supervisors, shifting attitudes, and understanding the hidden rules of business are a few outcomes Getting Ahead participants discuss in the following pages. Rather than telling you how your organization must change, it is my hope that the suggestions in this book will motivate you to find your own path to employee and business stability.

This book will explore how businesses can improve engagement, productivity, and financial returns using strategies that stabilize lower-wage employees who are living in daily instability. With a shift in mindset on the part of both the business and the employees, the new paradigm will create the sought-after stability businesses and employees need to thrive now and into the future.

Business Perspective

*"It drives us crazy! Employees will say,
'I can't come to work,' followed by, 'I need money.'"*

*"When employees are late or don't show up, it
creates a backlog in our workflow. It impacts
productivity, and it impacts the dollars."*

Employee Perspective

*"When I started this job, I was wearing jeans and
T-shirts. I told myself it was okay. There were days I had
meetings and needed to network with managers, and
I knew my clothes were not okay. But it wasn't in my
budget to purchase new clothes. How can I play the part
when I don't have the pieces and parts to do the job?"*

*"I grew up in poverty, I have a lack of education, and I've
been in and out of prison. I wanted to change, but I didn't
know how. I didn't understand normal business ways. The
culture in this office is very different from anything I had
known before. When I first got here, I felt alone."*

CHAPTER 1

Instability – What Does It Cost a Business?

Whether we admit it or not, many of us have preconceived notions about skin color, gender, height, introverts, extroverts, weight, marital status, and more. We judge individuals based on the school they went to, the car they drive, the neighborhood they live in, even their hobbies. And we do the same thing at work.

In the workplace we are concerned with racial and gender dynamics and discrimination, but rarely do we look at economic class and its impact on the success of the business operation. What causes daily instability anyway? Why does daily instability affect workplace performance, and how can we change our business operations to counteract the negative effects?

Each person is a tapestry woven from a unique set of experiences. These experiences come from the environment and the resources available. Employees from daily stability don't leave their experiences at the door when they enter the workplace, and neither do employees from daily instability. For the purposes of this book, I am adapting Ruby Payne's definition of poverty to describe the daily instability of some entry-level and lower-wage employees: Daily instability is the extent to which one does without resources. Survival in daily instability is difficult and takes a special set of skills, but those skills can cause problems if applied inappropriately in the workplace. What does that look like when the business world generally operates from a mindset of stability? The more resources people have, the better equipped they are to navigate systems and contribute professionally and personally. The environment we were raised in can affect the resources we have and how we use them. If employers understand the resources available to an employee, they can mentor that person into a stronger employee who contributes more.

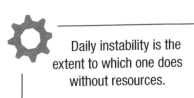

Daily instability is the extent to which one does without resources.

If you have picked up this book, chances are you are dealing with retention issues, human resources conflicts, workflow issues, absenteeism, and language barriers with entry-level, lower-wage employees. Operating in a global economy forces companies to squeeze more productivity, stability, and sustainability out of the business in the face of tight budgets and increased competition. All shareholders are looking for larger returns. How do businesses continue to provide a high level of client and customer experience while reducing expenses and improving the overall net income? How do companies make the owners and shareholders happy while doing all of this?

Research results from Bond and Galinsky at the Families and Work Institute indicate that 54% of low-wage employees are living in low-income households long term,[8] unlike, e.g., a college student working in a lower-wage position temporarily, often complemented by supports from a stable household. Perhaps conflicts rooted in socioeconomic differences have caused employers to fire or otherwise lose employees who could have made a great contribution to the company and the bottom line.

The few remarkable companies that grow consistently year after year and outpace their peers see one dominant theme emerge: a focus on talent. The most successful companies tend to appreciate, invest in, and value their employees. The leaders in these remarkable companies recognize that employee diversity, transparency, and sharing financial success with employees all help a company grow.

When employers invest in employees, the return on investment is employees who are motivated, engaged, and more productive. Team members who feel valued, trusted, and heard value the business more. When employees are included in decisions because they have expertise from working the job week after week, they take pride in their contributions to the team. When the business treats them well, employees treat the business well in return.

What Is Getting Ahead in the Workplace?

Getting Ahead is a program that helps employees investigate their economic reality and decide which resources to focus on improving.

Sherry, a youth guidance specialist supervisor and graduate of the Getting Ahead program, wishes her employer would provide incentives that make employees feel appreciated. Sherry isn't asking for much, just recognitions like employee of the month, certificates of achievement, and small gift cards. She says, "It would make people work harder and want to work harder." Echoing this sentiment, Renee Salazar, an emergency relief manager, says that if workers feel valued by an employer who encourages self-esteem, they will give their best.

In 2013 Gallup surveyed employees about their engagement and happiness. They reported that employee engagement leads to reduced absenteeism, lower turnover, less theft and lost merchandise, and fewer safety incidents. This, in turn, leads to higher customer loyalty, increased employee productivity, and enhanced profitability.

Engagement, productivity, loyalty, motivation, relationships—for employees in daily instability, they're all in some way shaped by that unstable environment. Relationships are a driving force for these employees. Many times their relationships with family, friends, and neighbors are their only assets. In the workplace, if companies don't create a relationship-based achievement model with employees, they will not get the engagement and productivity they need to keep the business profitable.

A Getting Ahead graduate named Amber said of her first professional office position, "I was respected, and my voice mattered for the first time." On the flip side Ellie, an employee coordinator, says her boss often uses "the parent voice" with her. This voice is the commanding voice parents use effectively with small children, but it leaves Ellie feeling empty and unmotivated. Voices, registers of language, and the language of negotiation are covered in more detail in Chapter 5. What's important here is that Ellie knows she must respect the manager's position even though she doesn't respect the manager. Amber is likely to work extra hard for her employer while Ellie—not so much.

Stability Paradigm

Stability Paradigm

Environment and Resources

Stability

Hidden Rules
Language
Engagement
Motivation

Opportunity

Retention, Performance, and Profits

In my talks with business leaders, one theme was abundantly clear: They are all looking for stability, and so are employees. If companies can stabilize employees, they will stabilize the business as a whole. In that process they create opportunities for both the business and the employees. By looking through the lens of economic class and examining how the employees' environment of daily instability can destabilize the business, an astute observer can spot internal changes that will open up areas of growth for the business.

Resources are not just money; they are a set of strengths that can be built upon. aha! Process's work defines 11 essential resources:

- **Financial** – Money to purchase goods and services.
- **Emotional** – Ability to control emotional responses.
- **Mental/Cognitive** – Mental capability to deal with daily life.
- **Language/Formal Register** – Ability to use appropriate vocabulary and grammar.
- **Social Capital/Support Systems** – Friends, family, and other resources to help in times of need.
- **Physical** – Physical health and mobility.
- **Spiritual** – Belief in divine purpose and guidance.
- **Integrity and Trust** – Trust, predictability, and safety.
- **Motivation and Persistence** – Energy, drive, and planning.
- **Relationships and Role Models** – Access to people who consistently behave appropriately and are nurturing.
- **Knowledge of Hidden Rules** – Knowing the unspoken cues and behaviors of different groups.

The more resources an employee has, the more opportunities that employee has to contribute at a higher level. When employees are living in daily instability and have been for generations, they will have some resources that are much stronger than others. The good news? We are all capable of growing all of our resources. Chapter 6 includes a more detailed discussion of resources.

"Hidden rules" are the unspoken cues and habits of a group.[9] As one fast food employee told me, "They are rules that are obvious to me but may not be obvious to you and vice versa." There are different hidden rules at work, at home, at social events, at sporting events—and there are different hidden rules in each economic class. When employees bring the hidden rules of daily instability to work, those rules can conflict with the hidden rules of the workplace and create misunderstandings between employees—especially between lower-wage employees and management. Chapter 4 will explore how hidden rules sometimes get in the way of productivity.

Businesses operate using mostly middle class hidden rules, but one economic class's hidden rules are not necessarily "better" than another's; all of the hidden rules are useful for survival and growth in the appropriate context. Since businesses operate using middle class norms to create a stable environment, this book examines in depth the differences between the hidden rules of daily stability and the hidden rules of daily instability. Daily stability gives people the ability to plan for tomorrow and the future, a necessity for a successful business.

The following checklists encourage thinking about the skills necessary to survive in daily instability, daily stability, and long-term stability. When you look at these assessments, ask yourself, "How is this different or similar to my experience, and which of these pieces, if any, affect stability, productivity, and business strategies in the workplace?"

Stability Assessments
Do you know how to operate in daily financial instability?

Put a check by each item that applies to you:

_____ 1. I know which of my friends and family have an extra couch or bed if I need a place to stay for a while.

_____ 2. I know where to find the cheapest and best-working Laundromat.

_____ 3. I rely primarily on reading body language and nonverbal cues.

_____ 4. I live without a checking account and credit cards.

_____ 5. I know where to go for help when I don't have money to pay the bills.

_____ 6. I can move in half a day without a truck.

_____ 7. I know how to get and use food stamps or an electronic benefits transfer card.

_____ 8. I have at least two places in town where I get phone charging and wireless Internet access without buying much or being asked to leave.

_____ 9. I have arranged my schedule to get to two jobs without the use of a car.

_____ 10. I can find another job quickly if my boss makes me mad and I quit.

_____ 11. I have asked for an advance on my paycheck.

_____ 12. I am comfortable using casual speech at work with my boss, coworkers, and customers.

_____ 13. I openly discuss disagreements I have with my boss and coworkers.

_____ 14. I have several friends and relatives who work here—that's how I got this job.

_____ 15. I have gone without work for periods of time and survived.

Total Points: _____

      0–3 = Can't operate

      4–7 = Inexperienced operator

      8–12 = Expert operator

Can you operate in this environment? Can you name any of your direct reports who do? Take a moment to think about an employee who is late or absent a lot or seems often to be getting into trouble with a supervisor, a coworker, or management. This is an employee you might be considering disciplining or letting go. Keep that person in mind as you continue through the concepts and strategies in this book. Not only will the book help you better understand that employee, it will help you understand yourself, your friends, and your business.

What is reality like when living without a checking account and working two jobs without the use of a car? In that position, a person is simply in survival mode, not planning for later today, let alone for tomorrow. This assessment gives a sense of the challenges employees might be struggling with on a daily basis.

Sonia Holycross, an education and family development coordinator who was recently promoted, says, "This environment [of daily instability] leaves employees in a whirlwind state that directly affects productivity, the quality of the products, and overall culture and expectations." Sonia's insights are especially valuable as she is a Getting Ahead graduate herself.

Do you know how to operate in daily financial stability?

Put a check by each item that applies to you:

_____ 1. I regularly get my children to Little League, piano lessons, and soccer.

_____ 2. I like to shop in my free time and frequently buy things online.

_____ 3. I regularly use a credit card, checking account, and savings account and know how to check and improve my credit score.

_____ 4. I assume my children are going to college and make financial and activity decisions to help ensure that happens.

_____ 5. I understand the difference among the principal, interest, and escrow statements on my house payment.

_____ 6. I volunteer for field trips and community service projects at my children's school and have never missed a parent/teacher conference.

_____ 7. I use my own home Internet access.

_____ 8. I have a favorite dry cleaner, pet groomer, and computer repair person.

_____ 9. I take at least one multi-day vacation each year and plan it well in advance.

_____ 10. I participate in professional development and training programs.

_____ 11. I use a time-management system and/or planner.

_____ 12. I can bite my tongue when my boss makes me mad.

_____ 13. I know how to do my work in ways that meet both my organization's needs and my personal goals.

_____ 14. I know the patterns of promotion within the organization and have a plan for how to attain my own promotion.

_____ 15. I know which subjects can and can't be discussed at work and regularly guide my behavior accordingly.

Total Points: _____

> **0–3** = Can't operate
>
> **4–7** = Inexperienced operator
>
> **8–12** = Expert operator

Can you operate in this environment? Employees from the environment of daily financial stability can easily pay for most things they need and want; they can keep things stable and are able to borrow money if needed. This environment is focused on achievement, and we will discuss that more in Chapter 2.

Of this environment, recently promoted employee Sonia says: "There is an emphasis on securing tomorrow while living out today's dreams and expectations."

Do you know how to operate in long-term financial stability?

Put a check by each item that applies to you:

_____ 1. I have a favorite restaurant in several different countries.

_____ 2. I have a financial advisor, lawyer, interior decorator, gardener, and I use a domestic employment service.

_____ 3. I have at least two residences.

_____ 4. I enroll my children in the preferred private schools.

_____ 5. I am on the boards of at least two charities or nonprofit organizations.

_____ 6. I support or buy the work of a particular artist.

_____ 7. I know how to make financial investment decisions by analyzing target stocks and my own financial position.

_____ 8. I buy things and make travel plans without checking the price.

_____ 9. I went to the same college my parent and grandparent attended and am planning for my child to do the same.

_____ 10. I have negotiated my employment contracts with the appropriate compensation and perks.

_____ 11. I know how to present our organization's financials so that we are seen in the best possible light.

_____ 12. I know how to protect and secure personal and organizational data.

_____ 13. I understand and know how to balance business imperatives for short-term profits and long-term goals.

_____ 14. I use my connections to establish business liaisons with other organizations.

Total Points: _____

      0–3 = Can't operate

      4–7 = Inexperienced operator

      8–12 = Expert operator

Can you or do you operate in this environment? Do you socialize with colleagues who do? Many times people living in long-term stability will delegate responsibility for their daily stability needs to paid staff—i.e., they use their earnings to have other people handle things for them so they can continue spending their time on connections. As a professional you know how to create and deliver presentations to the executives and owners of the company and how to present a report about money and earnings in the best light. This is often a difficult concept for employees on the front line who don't understand how the executive suite operates.

When I asked Sonia about her observations of long-term stability, she said, "I see there are trust issues in wealth and isolation as well, but over there you get called 'eccentric' while in daily instability you are considered an outcast."

It's not easy to survive in any of these environments. Those from stability are not well equipped to survive in daily instability, and those from daily instability are not well equipped to survive in stability. Because business norms are built on the hidden rules and required skills of daily and long-term stability, helping employees build stability in their own lives helps further stabilize and optimize the business as well.

What Instability Costs a Business

Recently an executive in wholesale frozen food distribution told me he wasn't concerned with the turnover of his entry-level employees. He said he loses a lot of them, but he can hire replacements at that skill level any day of the week. Why does he choose to remain on that "turnover treadmill" rather than increasing productivity and competitive advantage by building stability for long-term employees? Once a pattern is established, it is very hard to break that pattern. When an "expendable" employee quits, there is a very good chance the company will hire someone with the same work patterns as the employee who just walked off the job.

On the other hand, Susan Chrisman, the owner/operator of several nationally franchised fast food restaurants, saw what turnover was costing her businesses and decided to try a different model. After implementing strategies from Bridges, she has pushed her overall measured satisfaction score past the national chain average. Her 90-day turnover rate dropped to 27% less than the national average as well. Best of all, the change in employee culture from "expendable" to "career" attracts candidates for new openings who are looking to build stability for the long term.

As far back as 2004, researchers from the Boston College Center for Work and Family predicted that "the value of hourly and lower-wage employees to many organizations is only expected to increase in the future. Demographic changes in the United States workforce mean that traditional sources of qualified personnel are less likely to provide an adequate number of skilled entry-level workers … In order to stay competitive in an increasingly global economy, employers will need to hire, train, and retain entry-level personnel."[10] Those predictions were entirely correct, and each fiscal year the need for retention of qualified personnel increases. Innovative approaches like Susan's, in which employees' resources and skills are built up over time, have proven themselves to be the best (and most profitable!) practices in the 21st-century economy.

When the Society for Human Resource Management (SHRM) partnered with The Economist Intelligence Unit to look at future human resources trends, these were the main takeaways from the report:

- Economic demographics, including the aging out of the baby boomers, will result in a young population of employees that might pose additional challenges for business leaders.

- Lack of opportunities may lead to a declining labor force, and that labor force will most likely not have the level of education employers seek. As the report explains, "globalization has allowed companies to look for cheaper labor elsewhere, and the focus on shareholder value has led to pressure for higher profits. This pressure on wages is likely to continue, resulting in lower expectations from workers and possibly to reduced expenditure by individuals on education."[11]

- Currently there are disconnects between business needs and the areas of technology, engineering, and emotional intelligence. When coupled with the shift in demographics, additional internal training programs will need to be added within the business to bridge the gap between business demands and the knowledge level of the employees.

- Economic and generational differences will require businesses to provide new employee leadership strategies that keep the company viable in highly competitive global markets.

- With workplace flexibility and remote working on the rise, businesses will need to find leadership strategies that maximize productivity and minimize differences of time zones, cultures, and patterns created by economic class differences.

- More and more routine tasks are being automated, so management is always searching for skilled employees. The gap between automatable tasks and skilled employees will continue to grow, and as inequality increases, there is concern about social and political stability. This will require businesses to spend more time training, supporting, and retaining their workforces.[12]

All of these trends indicate that employers will need to spend more time training, educating, and mentoring staff members to help them build resources and stability. Creating partnerships to provide resources for employees that businesses alone cannot provide is one stability-building strategy.

Rhino Foods, an ice cream maker, cut their employee turnover rate by more than half. They attribute this success to the leadership at Rhino Foods participating in a regional resource network for employers. The United Way of Chittenden County, which coordinates the efforts of the resource network, reported Rhino's savings in turnover costs to be $164,500—as well as saving 47 jobs.[13]

It does pay to stabilize. What is the instability of the workforce costing your business?

Return on Stability Initiatives Analysis

Instability, in the form of turnover and lost productivity, is costing businesses money. Companies that take the time to review what instability can look like might find that they can afford more stability initiatives within the business than they might have predicted. For instance, strategies like simplifying the application and onboarding process can be implemented at little or no cost.

Employee turnover is one of the biggest drains on productivity and profits, but if your company hasn't yet taken the time to review all of the hard and soft costs of employee turnover, don't worry. We'll use a cost of turnover worksheet from SHRM to look at two sample businesses first.

The first sample business is a regional restaurant corporation consisting of fine dining and fast food restaurants. The company worked to achieve a 100% employee turnover rate in an industry that often sees 200% turnover.

Cost of Turnover Spreadsheet

ESSENTIAL DATA

Employee's Classification	Hourly, entry-level crew, supervisors (support supervisors—like leads), hostesses, cooks, dishwashers, servers—in fast food and full service restaurants
Employee's hourly pay rate:	$8
Employee's supervisor pay rate:	$12
Corporate office staff pay rate (average):	$15

HARD COSTS	Hours	Wages	Total
Pre-Departure			
Separation processing Administrative time	1	$22	$22
Vacancy Costs			
Coworker burden Overtime: Added shifts	0	$0	$0
Hiring search firm or temp agency	0	$0	$0
Developing advertisement(s) Administrative time	1	$22	$22
Placing advertisement Cost of advertising space(s)			$0
Selection and Sign-On			
Interviewing	3	$15	$45
Reference checking	1	$15	$15
Drug testing/psychological testing			$0
Orientation	2	$15	$30
On-the-job training	40	$8	$320
Uniforms			$50
TOTAL Hard Costs of Turnover			**$504**

Cost of Turnover Spreadsheet (continued)

SOFT COSTS	Hours	Wages	Total
Pre-Departure			
Lost productivity of departing employee Exiting employee performance at 50–75%	120	$8	$960
Lost productivity of coworkers	30	$8	$240
Increased time discussing departure and organizational conditions	2	$15	$30
Increased workload for employees	0	$8	$0
Lost productivity of supervisor	0	$15	$0
During Vacancy			
Lost productivity of vacant position Overtime Added shifts	0	$8	$0
Lost productivity of supervisor Time spent filling in	0	$15	$0
Recruiting administration Supervisor's time with schedule changes/overtime	1	$15	$15
Selection and Sign-On			
Lost productivity during training Replacement requires support/ direction	20	$8	$160
Lost productivity of coworkers Existing employees distracted	10	$8	$80
Lost productivity of supervisor	1	$15	$15
TOTAL Soft Costs of Turnover			**$1,500**

Cost of Turnover Spreadsheet (continued)

TOTAL COST OF TURNING OVER Hard and Soft Costs	1 employee	**$2,004**

TOTAL COST OF TURNING OVER Hard and Soft Costs	10 employees	**$20,040**

FORMULA FOR ANNUAL TURNOVER COST			
	# of employees	**Cost of turnover (hard and soft) per employee**	
Number of exiting employees	425	$2,004	$851,700

Society for Human Rights Management. (2015). Turnover: Cost-of-turnover worksheet. SHRM. Retrieved from http://www.shrm.org/templatestools/samples/hrforms/articles/pages/1cms_011163.aspx. Used with permission.

This particular company found this exercise very eye opening. They expected (yet underestimated) the hard costs of turnover—the administrative time, separation processing, vacancy costs, interviewing, onboarding, training—and they hadn't even considered the soft costs: lost productivity before and after a person terminates, as well as the lost productivity in getting a new employee up to speed in the role. Turnover affects more than just the departing employee; other team members, supervisors, and human resources personnel also bear a burden when an employee leaves or is let go. Everything done to stabilize employees' lives will improve retention, save money, and stabilize the business operation.

In this next scenario a manufacturer hires an average of 100 employees per year and loses 84% of those employees before the year is over.

Cost of Turnover Spreadsheet

ESSENTIAL DATA

Employee's Classification	Production
Employee's hourly pay rate:	$8
Employee's supervisor pay rate:	$12
Corporate office staff pay rate (average):	$15

HARD COSTS	Hours	Wages	Total
Pre-Departure			
Separation processing Administrative time	3	$12	$36
Vacancy Costs			
Coworker burden Overtime: Added shifts	6	$15	$90
Hiring search firm or temp agency	0	$15	$0
Developing advertisement(s) Administrative time	1	$15	$15
Placing advertisement Cost of advertising space(s)			$200
Selection and Sign-On			
Interviewing	3	$15	$45
Reference checking	5	$15	$75
Drug testing/psychological testing			$0
Orientation and on-the-job training	6	$15	$90
TOTAL Hard Costs of Turnover			**$551**

Cost of Turnover Spreadsheet (continued)

SOFT COSTS	Hours	Wages	Total
Pre-Departure			
Lost productivity of departing employee Exiting employee performance at 50–75%	20	$8	$160
Lost productivity of coworkers	8	$8	$64
Increased time discussing departure and organizational conditions	4	$12	$48
Increased workload for employees	20	$8	$160
Lost productivity of supervisor	15	$12	$180
During Vacancy			
Lost productivity of vacant position Overtime Added shifts	20	$8	$160
Lost productivity of supervisor Time spent filling in	20	$12	$240
Recruiting administration Supervisor's time with schedule changes/overtime	5	$12	$60
Selection and Sign-On			
Lost productivity during training Replacement requires support/direction	80	$8	$640
Lost productivity of coworkers Existing employees distracted	160	$8	$1,280
Lost productivity of supervisor	20	$12	$240
TOTAL Soft Costs of Turnover			**$3,232**

Cost of Turnover Spreadsheet (continued)

TOTAL COST OF TURNING OVER Hard and Soft Costs	1 employee	**$3,783**

TOTAL COST OF TURNING OVER Hard and Soft Costs	10 employees	**$37,830**

FORMULA FOR ANNUAL TURNOVER COST		
	# of employees	**Cost of turnover (hard and soft) per employee**	
Number of exiting employees	84	$3,783	$317,772

Employee turnover continues to cost this company more than a quarter million dollars each year. Think of the ways that money could be spent to stabilize employees, reduce turnover, increase productivity, and boost the net income of the business. Why should a company spend time on the turnover treadmill when it could be spending that time honing strategic initiatives?

Cost of Turnover

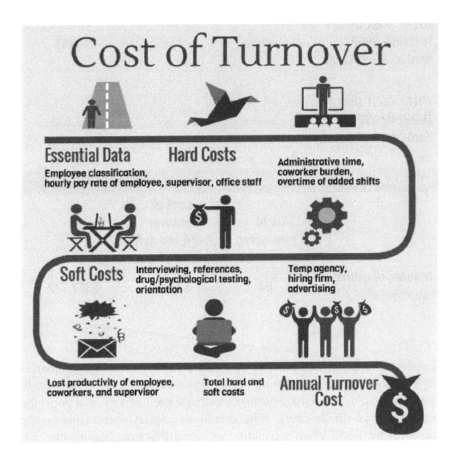

According to Ross Blake, SHRM estimates a cost of $3,500 to replace an $8-per-hour employee, and SHRM's figure was the lowest of 17 companies that reported on the cost. Other companies reported that turnover cost between 30% and 50% of the annual salary of entry-level employees.[14] For a full-time employee at $8 an hour, the higher turnover cost is $5,000–$8,000 per employee based on the 30–50% metric.

After crunching her own numbers, Susan Chrisman reports that her turnover costs per person are $2,179. In fiscal year 2014 this amounted to $392,220. A recent conversation with a human resources manager revealed that the turnover cost at her firm was well over $11,000 per person. You only need to plug your numbers into the worksheet to see how much money is being wasted—but you might want to wait until you're sitting down!

No matter what the turnover cost is per employee or per year, the point is it pays to stabilize, retain, and promote employees from within. The actual savings are relative to the size of the business, market share, and sales, but the money saved can be used to implement further stability initiatives based on the cost of turnover. The SOURCE, a regional resource network for employers in Grand Rapids, Michigan, estimates that a typical return on investment (ROI) for a business participating in a resource network is 150–200%.[15] The most recent annual report from the Schenectady Area and Capital Region Employer Resource Network, a member of the national ERN-USA, indicates an average ROI of 231% with an average retention rate of 89% across 20 employers from various sectors.[16] That's 89% *retention,* not turnover!

Managing employees takes time. Absenteeism, often a first sign of turnover in the making, affects productivity, morale, work schedules, and workloads. It affects deadlines and potentially requires other employees to work overtime. That increases costs. Some companies move to scheduling software that allows them to track schedules and absenteeism, enabling supervisors and managers to see employee patterns. Many resource network models include plans for a resource specialist to intervene immediately when an employee has an unexcused absence or tardiness. Whatever the barrier is, it can often be dealt with that day. With or without software, detecting early warning signs allows a manager to mentor employees and thereby retain talent.

Sonia, if you'll recall, is a Getting Ahead graduate who was recently promoted, but she grew up in daily instability. She moved frequently, was in a gang, used drugs heavily, and by her own telling her life was miserable. After examining her own economic class experience through Getting Ahead, she found what drives her achievement. She says, "I can have mutual respect for a company or business because we value the same things now: hard work, mutual respect, and a sense of safety that comes from the feeling of steady employment." Sonia will be the first to say that she has moved beyond stabilization into a sense of thriving—her life now is rich personally and professionally.

Many companies assume that entry-level, lower-wage employees are expendable, easy to replace, and have little effect on the company's performance. Why should they invest time and money in them? Heymann and Barrera, in the book *Profit at the Bottom of the Ladder: Creating Value by Investing in Your Workforce,* focused on understanding the outcomes and experiences of companies that do invest in entry-level employees. Not only did they discover that it is possible to provide better working conditions *and* be profitable, they learned that the companies providing better working conditions for employees "at the bottom of the ladder" actually increased their profits.

This chapter has explored the costs of employee turnover and other problems that can arise for employees from daily instability. The next chapter will delve deeper into what the environments of daily stability and daily instability look like.

Business Perspective

"These are my biggest issues: absenteeism, work adherence, work ethic, and behaviors. It appears that low-wage employees just don't care."

"Before Bridges, I would have said that entry-level, low-wage employees are lazy, not dependable, and takers. After Bridges, I shifted my paradigm. I realized my thinking about this was all wrong."

Employee Perspective

"Knowing the mental model for poverty helps me take the emotion out of the situation and problem solve where I have control. That brings less stress for me in the workplace. It helps me balance personal chaos and allows me to give more of me and be more productive at work."

"When I was unemployed, I cut my own hair. Now I know that potential employers make a decision about me in the first 30 seconds, but sometimes I still can't afford to pay $22 for a haircut."

"Growing up in middle class, I never understood why our neighbor piled up her trash behind the house. Now I'm in situational poverty, and I understand why because I had to do the same thing. I could not afford waste management fees."

CHAPTER 2

What Can Daily Instability and Daily Stability Look Like?

Ruby Payne has written that "knowledge bases are a form of privilege, just as social access and money are,"[17] and "how you spend your time impacts your knowledge base and resources."[18] If there are entry-level, low-wage employees on the team, some probably come from unstable economic environments. Phil DeVol, creator of the Getting Ahead books and courses, asked 50 individuals who were living in poverty how they spent their time. The mental model for daily instability on the next page shows the concerns, priorities, and challenges of people whose day-to-day lives aren't stable. Mental models are tools that help the mind store abstract information. This mental model is a visual representation of how employees in daily instability spend their time based on their environment. In turn, this environment shapes the knowledge base that people from instability bring to the workplace. Relationships are central to the mental model because they are the key asset and driving force for people living in daily instability. This mental model is especially important because it was generated directly from the lived experience of instability, but remember that these patterns are not true for everyone, and they should not be used to stereotype or create/reinforce prejudice.

Mental Model for Daily Instability

This mental model shows us the concerns of individuals in daily instability, and any of these components can contribute to the instability. Relationships are central because people in daily instability rely on each other to address the other concerns in the circle. Because so many of the concerns are about meeting immediate needs, it is easy to understand how instability forces people to live in "the tyranny of the moment." This leaves little time for future planning. Many times having a future picture serves as a motivator or coping strategy. Individuals in instability are dealing with the problems of the day and miss out on these benefits because there is no time to plan for the future.

A future story often serves as a motivation or a coping strategy for an employee in the workplace, particularly when working relationships with supervisors and other employees—or even the job assignments—are not fulfilling or rewarding. If employees can focus on aspects of the job that relate to what they want to do professionally, this can help keep them motivated in lower-wage positions while they work toward promotion.

Mental Model for Instability: What It's Like Now

Adapted from *Getting Ahead in a Just-Gettin'-By World* (DeVol, 2015a)

"Agency time" may be an unfamiliar concept to some readers. Even while working, the average householder living in daily instability spends a significant amount of time seeking agency support for basic needs like food, rent, and utilities—necessities that people living in a stable environment often take for granted. Carol Steegman, who is working full time as an office coordinator and building her resources, told me she spent about 20 hours a month seeking help from various agencies, including food stamps, food banks, Medicaid, WIC, legal aid, dental clinic, childcare support, utilities and rent assistance, and Salvation Army.

Sonia, a former lower-wage employee recently promoted, told me the hardest thing about working with an agency when she was living in the tyranny of the moment was managing the strict requirements of paperwork when her life felt chaotic and messy. Carol once moved 12 times in four years, often staying with friends and family; people in situations like this often don't have an organized system for storing identification and other documents—theirs or their children's. Agencies often require supporting documentation from employers, which can hold up much-needed benefits. People who work during regular business hours are out of luck because that's also when the agencies are open. Taking time off work to seek assistance means employees don't get paid for that time, and to an employer it looks like they don't care about the job. As Sonia said, this "leaves the employee with a great sense of hopelessness."

What happens in the tyranny of the moment is that a crisis in one area tends to affect other areas until the crisis snowballs into something unmanageable.

Take transportation, for example. When people live with daily uncertainty, many times they do not have reliable vehicles if they have them at all. A Getting Ahead graduate named Roberta shared the following example of this. Her car broke down, and she didn't have the resources to call a tow truck or get the repairs done. This meant Roberta couldn't take her three children to preschool, kindergarten, and middle school, and by the time she found them rides, she couldn't possibly get to work on time. Last week her boss told her if she was late one more time she was fired, so Roberta is thinking she won't even call in. She is pretty sure she can't stop bad things from happening to her.

Roberta, now jobless, asks a friend to watch her children so she can get to a temp agency to find work somewhere else. The friend watches the kids, and the agency gets Roberta set up with a temporary job starting the next day. When Roberta gets home, the friend asks her to return the favor and watch her kids tomorrow.

No matter where Roberta turns, she faces a dilemma. Will she go to the new job, or will she watch her friend's kids? Most likely she will watch her friend's kids. Why? Because her friend watched her kids while she went to the agency the day before. Because relationships are the main driving force in daily instability, Roberta and her friend "have each other's backs."

Roberta's reasons for not showing up for work are complicated and due largely to circumstances beyond her control, but when she's tried to explain similar situations in the past, she's been told to quit making up excuses. What do Roberta's employer and the temp agency see, then? Just another "no-show no-call," an irresponsible or lazy person who didn't come to work.

As I've said, when one lives in daily instability, the driving force is relationships. Roberta and others like her must rely first on family and friends to meet needs that cannot be met with financial resources. Many times people swap services like childcare, eldercare, and transportation to mediate crises. Individuals in these circumstances often have difficulty envisioning and working realistic future stories for their lives; they are in survival mode, and relationships with friends and family are the only insurance policies they hold.

The mental model for daily instability clearly indicates that time is spent providing for today, not for tomorrow. Whether it is dealing with where and how food will be secured, getting to and from work, safety, or finding and keeping housing, the reactive problem solving is for immediate needs only.

Daily instability can be painful. The more employers understand the "why" of this environment, the more they can understand the differences between the employees' environment and the environment of stability employers strive to create in the workplace. Understanding these differences has the ability to reduce conflict within the workplace.

Years ago I managed a software support call center. I had an employee who always took his earned time off as soon as he accumulated it. He lived in the tyranny of the moment and often had to leave work to "put out fires" at home or visit agencies for extra support. He was not able to process that he might need to plan for time off in the future. As it happened, he had a sudden illness that required bed rest for a week. Since he didn't have any sick or personal time banked, not only did it hit him hard financially, he nearly lost his job. The reality is that employees with unstable financial conditions are "more likely to change jobs frequently, often due to the challenges they face when balancing work and family responsibilities."[19] Simply stated, many times employees are forced to leave their jobs because they are busy meeting concrete, immediate needs and don't plan for abstract, future needs.

Marvin Green, a machinist, told me that before he understood this distinction between concrete, immediate thinking and abstract, future-oriented thinking, he was unable to develop a relationship with his boss. While Marvin attempted to communicate on a concrete level, his boss wanted him to share a longer, more abstract view of their work. It was through his exploration of economic class that Marvin made this discovery and used it to become a better communicator and therefore a higher-producing employee.

Many qualities of individuals from daily instability can be great assets when translated effectively to the workplace. It is worth noting that individuals in daily instability are great problem solvers—they are solving life problems every day. It is important for employers to recognize and utilize line workers' problem solving skills to improve the efficiency of operations, either by increasing the quality or the pace of production. These team members work the line each day, and they are problem solvers as well as persistent thinkers with strong willpower. Sometimes employers fail to see the qualities employees have. They see only the employees who are causing problems in attendance or performance. Employers see the problems, but they don't see the strengths within employees. The graphic below presents many positive qualities employers see (or overlook) as they work with individuals coming from generations of living in daily instability.

© ReginaSpeaking LLC

Causes of Daily Instability

So far I have discussed some ways daily instability affects employees and their work, but a question arises when we look at the mental model for daily instability: Is this all the employees' fault? The short answer is no.

Research into economic class and the causes of daily instability tends to focus on four areas. Behaviors of the individual are only one reason people stay in daily instability. Other areas of research focus are human and social capital in the community, exploitation, and political and economic structures. Each area of research is valid and covers factors that are known to perpetuate instability. As you look over the causes of poverty, you'll probably find one or two that resonate more deeply with you than the others, and that's great. Communities, businesses, institutions, and individuals are better served when people from every mindset are invited to the table to discuss instability. It is not an either/or situation; it's a both/and situation.

Behaviors of the Individual

Truly, everyone has made mistakes. Each mistake has cost time, money, opportunity, and maybe even a relationship or two. Individuals who experience instability on a daily level, who are solving problems for this very moment—they make mistakes too. And that keeps them in instability. When I spoke with Ermina Soler, who has lifted herself up and off the streets and into a stable job, she told me that she takes responsibility for the poor personal choices she made that contributed to her homelessness. Personal choices, however, are just one piece of the puzzle.

Human and Social Capital

The resources available to individuals, communities, and business can hold individuals in instability. Society tends to discount people who live in instability, and it discounts their friends too. LeLinda Ingram, a supervisor on the rise, told me she never tried to build relationships in the community because she didn't believe there was anything in it for her. Her mindset was that no one was going to help her. Because she thought she lacked access to social capital that could help her build bridges out of her daily instability, she stayed in that instability longer than she had to. It was the information she gained in Getting Ahead that shifted her mindset.

Building the resources of all creates a more sustainable community for businesses to operate in. By providing good-paying jobs, quality education, and sustainability where all live well instead of racism, discrimination, and jobs that don't pay well (when there are jobs at all), communities serve themselves well for this and future generations.

Exploitation

The research on exploitation as a cause of daily instability focuses on ways in which people in daily instability are taken advantage of because of their increased susceptibility due to the tyranny of the moment. Payday loans, rent-to-own agreements, auto financing with high interest rates, the drug trade, even keeping workers at 30 hours a week or less to avoid paying them benefits—these are all forms of exploitation. When people live in daily instability, they are living in the moment and not thinking much about how decisions will affect the future. Exploitive businesses rely on individuals who are focused on solving problems in the moment rather than looking forward to future ramifications. This exploitation perpetuates instability.

Political and Economic Structures

Lastly, political and economic structures can actually keep people in instability too. Political and social policies at the local, state, federal, and international levels keep groups and individuals in financial instability and benefit others with influence. Some examples include lobbying in Washington for bills that will influence industries and businesses, the global job market, and deindustrialization of small communities.

It is important for businesses to understand the bigger picture in which their employees are operating; making the transition out of daily instability is not just a matter of making better personal choices that will create stability. Each of the four causes of instability listed above plays a role in holding people back from getting out. The community in which a business resides may have some work to do to help build resources and eliminate barriers to hard work and success. Employers all around the country are finding ways to help their employees build resources and stabilize their lives rather than just asking employees to make changes themselves.

Causes of Poverty

Behaviors of the Individual	Human and Social Capital in the Community
Definition: *Research on the choices, behaviors, characteristics, and habits of people in poverty*	**Definition:** *Research on the resources available to individuals, communities, and businesses*
Sample topics: Dependence on welfare Morality Crime Single parenthood Breakup of families Intergenerational character traits Work ethic Racism and discrimination Commitment to achievement Spending habits Addiction, mental illness, domestic violence Planning skills Orientation to the future Language experience	**Sample topics:** Intellectual capital Social capital Availability of jobs Availability of well-paying jobs Racism and discrimination Availability and quality of education Adequate skill sets Childcare for working families Decline in neighborhoods Decline in social morality Urbanization Suburbanization of manufacturing Middle class flight City and regional planning

Exploitation	Political/Economic Structures
Definition: *Research on how people in poverty are exploited because they are in poverty*	**Definition:** *Research on the economic, political, and social policies at the international, national, state, and local levels*
Sample topics: Drug trade Racism and discrimination Payday lenders Subprime lenders Lease/purchase outlets Gambling Temp work Sweatshops Sex trade Internet scams	**Sample topics:** Globalization Equity and growth Corporate influence on legislators Declining middle class Deindustrialization Job loss Decline of unions Taxation patterns Salary ratio of CEO to line worker Immigration patterns Economic disparity Racism and discrimination

Source: DeVol, P. E. (2015a). *Getting ahead in a just-gettin'-by world* (3rd rev. ed.). Highlands, TX: aha! Process.

In the book *Bridges to Sustainable Communities,* Phil DeVol outlines concrete and abstract knowledge in relation to all of the elements within the mental model for daily instability. I have taken it a step further to outline what pain points those elements are creating for the business operation. It isn't the business's pain alone, though. It is also the pain of those living in daily instability.

Business and Employee Pains Caused by the Environment of Daily Instability[20]

Element	Concrete Knowledge	Abstract Knowledge
Transportation	Vehicles are not dependable and require constant repair; breakdowns result in lost jobs, missed appointments, and stress. Insufficient public transportation limits mobility.	Cars purchased "as is" from buy-here, pay-here dealers come with interest rates as high as 15.5%.[21]
Housing	Houses are often in isolated rural areas or unsafe urban and suburban neighborhoods. Houses are crowded, people come and go, there is no private place for children to do their homework, rooms are used for many purposes, people sleep on the couch, repairs can't be made, landlord can be difficult, people have to move frequently.	The majority of people in poverty spend at least 50% of their income on housing; nearly a quarter pay more than 70%.[22] Affordable rental units have been on the decline since the 1970s. Federal support for low-income housing fell 49% between 1980 and 2003.[23]
Jobs	Jobs don't pay enough, temp work doesn't provide enough hours or benefits, many work two jobs to make ends meet, no vacation. Money is a constant worry. People are vulnerable to the prices of gas and milk going up by the gallon.	Proportion of unemployed workers looking for a job for 27 weeks or more: 23%, highest proportion in 20 years.[24] "Most available jobs had three unhappy traits: They paid low wages, offered no benefits, and led nowhere."[25]

Business Pain	Employee Pain
Turnover, tardiness, absenteeism.	Price of gas, walk to bus stop, bus lines don't run at the correct time or to the best destinations for the job, multiple buses needed, lack of reliable transportation, upkeep on cars.
Lack of sleep may affect productivity, human resources issues with changes of address.	Unstable housing options, multiple families in house, inability to pay rent, dollars spent on rent, predatory mortgage lenders.
Turnover grind—employee continues to seek better-paying jobs with benefits, steady and consistent hours.	Low wages, inconsistent hours, multiple jobs, part-time, temp jobs, no maternity leave, no paid vacation, boring work.

(continued on next page)

Business and Employee Pains Caused
by the Environment of Daily Instability (continued)

Element	Concrete Knowledge	Abstract Knowledge
Health	Being sick, caring for others who are sick, and trying to get healthcare are time consuming and exhausting.	Poverty is associated with increased risks of cardiovascular disease, respiratory disease, ulcers, rheumatoid disorders, psychiatric diseases, and a number of types of cancer.[26]
Children	It's hard to get kids through the day; people have concerns about school, health, clothing, and safety. Childcare arrangements are unreliable, while good childcare is either unavailable or too expensive.	"There are many more poor children in the United States than in most Western European countries. In the United States, one-fifth of all children live below the poverty level."[27] Forty-five percent of all children live in low-income families, and one in five lives in a poor family.[28]
Safety	Protecting your people and yourself is a constant concern. The criminal justice system is part of life; members of the family are in jail, on parole, or on probation. The drug culture is threatening.	Prison population: one in 143 adults in prison, an all-time high.[29] Sixty to seventy percent of people in prison are from poverty.
Family and Friends	Relationships are important. They are a resource needed for survival.	"Inner-city social networks are not nearly as dense or effective as those Stack found in the late 1960s, for like the sprawling suburbs and small villages in the heartland, inner cities too have less social capital nowadays than they once did."[30] "Individuals who grow up in socially isolated rural and inner-city areas are held back, not merely because they tend to be financially and educationally deprived, but also because they are relatively poor in social ties that can provide a 'hand up.'"[31]

Business Pain	Employee Pain
Time off for self and children, lack of motivation and productivity—exhausted.	No health insurance, poor quality of food, sleep deprivation, hard physical labor, unreliable transportation to get to health services, lack of support system for sick children, eldercare, lack of money.
Absenteeism due to unreliable childcare.	Poor quality of food, fewer after-school activities, no time to help with homework, unreliable childcare, lack of money.
Relationships take precedence over work.	Victims of predatory lending, victims of street crime, drug trade, sex trade, relationships take precedence over work.
Relationships take precedence over work.	Relationships needed for survival, take precedence over work.

(continued on next page)

Business and Employee Pains Caused
by the Environment of Daily Instability (continued)

Element	Concrete Knowledge	Abstract Knowledge
Entertainment	Entertainment takes many forms, including cable television, video games, drugs, alcohol, music, and spending time with friends.	Entertainment is a driving force for people in poverty. It helps them survive a very stressful life.
Agency Time	People in poverty typically go to 3–9 agencies in the course of a year to get needs addressed. Each agency demands behavioral changes, a plan of action, and time for the activities listed in the plan.	"Much of human life consists of playing ... roles within specific institutions ... Individuals' chances of interacting with any given kind of institution are not random: Families from elite backgrounds tend to participate in institutions serving the elite, and families in poverty tend to be involved in institutions serving the poor ... Children grow up within a broad, highly stratified social system."[32]
Food	There are concerns about not having enough. Grocery stores have moved out of the neighborhood. Local grocery stores that stayed overcharge, and the quality of produce is poor. Many must buy from convenience stores. Fast food outlets provide relatively cheap but fattening food.	"Twenty-three percent of the nation's lower-income classes are obese, compared with 16% of the middle and upper classes ... Large supermarket chains (the best bet for affordable, fresh, and healthy foods) abandoned less affluent city neighborhoods, focusing instead on the suburbs ... There are three times as many supermarkets in wealthy neighborhoods as in poor ones, according to a 2002 study in the *American Journal of Preventive Medicine*."[33] "Low-income ZIP codes have 30% more convenience stores, which tend to lack healthy items, than middle income ZIP codes."[34]

Business Pain	Employee Pain
Preferred forms foster little bridging social capital, humor may offend.	Decreased networking capacity, strained social events, harassment complaints.
Absenteeism, life/work balance issues.	Life/work balance to make ends meet, services based on middle class environment.
Turnover, tardiness, absenteeism.	Food insecurity, poor-quality food, fast food, highly processed food—leads to illness, diabetes, obesity.

With a better understanding of the environment of daily instability and the pain it can bring to the workplace, employers can shift their ways of doing business to get the results they are looking for.

> So far this book has been strategizing from an employer's perspective, but it is also important to look at how the community is impacting poverty. The additional question that needs to be acted on is: What can the community do to stabilize citizens? Cascade Engineering is a classic example of getting involved in the community to create sustainability at a higher level. Get involved with local nonprofits and workforce development and economic development groups to make it happen.

Mental Model for Daily Stability

In contrast to the mental model that shows what life in daily instability looks like, let's see what a mental model for daily stability looks like.

When people have a stable financial environment, the mental model looks different from the mental model for daily instability. Instead of relationships, achievement is the driving force. People in daily stability are planning for tomorrow, planning for retirement, putting their kids in private lessons, and planning their next vacation. People living in daily stability don't depend on relationships to help them make it through today. Furthermore, a crisis in one aspect of the circle doesn't spill over and cause a crisis in other parts. If the car breaks down, people in daily stability are able to solve the problem before it causes others. They take a taxi, rent a car for the duration of the repair, or use the second or third car that is in the driveway or garage.

Employees living in daily stability are interested in issues of prevention, they have a career rather than just a job, they are thinking about retirement, vacations—and all of this implies that a future story is happening here. Entertainment isn't given a special thought because it is part of life; it's already built in and assumed. Those living in middle class are usually planning for the future, working towards accomplishing that future story that an achievement-based mindset and lifestyle values.

Take a moment to look at the two mental models and notice where employees spend their time when they are dealing with daily instability versus where employees spend their time when they have financial stability. The stability circle may also represent the filter you are looking through as you

Mental Model for Stability

Adapted from *Getting Ahead in a Just-Gettin'-By World* (DeVol, 2015a)

observe and work beside employees. You may be looking at employees who are experiencing a lot of instability in their lives, and as a manager, you may even be asking: Why can't that employee just "buck up" like everyone else does around here? What you are really asking is: Why can't this employee be more like me?

Looking at employees through the lens of economic class makes business sense, but employers have to be sure to put aside their own class biases to get the return on investment. By better understanding the workforce that comes from daily economic instability, employers can better stabilize the workforce, boost productivity, and increase the income of the business.

One last caution or comment about these mental models: It is important to note that these circles do not represent specific people; they represent environments in which individuals operate. Environments impact people differently, and people impact environments differently. These ideas are about environments and patterns, and there are always exceptions.

Mental Model for Long-Term Stability

The mental model for long-term stability is quite different from the other two, and there are understandably fewer people who live this experience. This mental model represents the daily environment of the business owners, investors, C-suite executives, and high-producing sales executives.

What is most apparent in this mental model? Stability, time horizon, problem solving strategies, and power look different than they do in the other two models. In this mental model the needs of the individual are taken care of today, tomorrow, next year—the time horizon extends to decades, generations. Connections are at the center of this model because in long-term stability, it isn't *what* you know as much as *who* you know.

Mental Model for Long-Term Stability

Adapted from *A Framework for Understanding Poverty* (Payne, 2013)

Privacy and maintenance of family traditions are expected and highly valued in long-term stability. People who have long-term stability also have the power to influence others and shape political policies and community direction.

The environment of daily instability is so unstable, employees who cope with it have to focus on solving immediate, concrete problems. As a result, they live mainly in the present. The environment of employees with daily stability is more predictable; employees have today covered, and they worry about the future. The planning horizon of those in daily stability is 2–4 years; people can make plans 2–4 years in advance and reasonably expect to see them through. For the most part, this is the perspective that shapes the daily operations of a business, though most businesses strive for long-term stability. The environment of those with wealth, or those with long-term stability, is so stable that they don't worry about today or tomorrow; they plan for future generations. The time horizon of long-term stability is up to two decades.

Mental Model for Business Instability

You have examined mental models for the experiences of individuals operating in varying levels of stability; now let's examine mental models for different levels of business stability. Businesses often experience varying levels of stability and instability that affect employee retention, organizational performance, and company profits, to name a few.

On a scale from one to five, rate the attendance of the company's employees. Does the business experience unscheduled absences or reliable attendance? Would you rate your department differently than the organization as a whole? Has the company investigated the causes of attendance problems? Is there money for research and development with continual investment back into new products and services for sustainability? If not, this is a strong indicator that the business is in its own tyranny of the moment and may have trouble stabilizing itself, let alone the employee base.

Features of the environment of business instability might be declining sales, loss of market share, poor leadership, changing trends, outdated technology or ideas, even a down market for a commodity company. Many business patterns create chaos, dysfunction, and cause businesses themselves to operate in the tyranny of the moment. Businesses experiencing instability share many problems with their employees from instability because they must focus on surviving the day with little or no equity to plan for the future. Luckily, if these businesses put some effort toward stabilizing the lives of their employees, they'll see an increase in the stability of the business as a whole.

Mental Model for Business Stability

Contrast those business instability problems with the concerns of a company that is growing, producing desirable products and solutions, staying competitive, building financial reserves, encouraging strong leadership, engaging in robust research and development, investing in great talent, and constantly honing a strategic plan for the future. That company is thinking about retaining employees, promoting talent from within, increasing productivity, and more, as evidenced in the mental model for business stability.

I wrote earlier about employee productivity, motivation, and engagement. What is your organization like? Is it a democracy or a dictatorship? Are employees able to contribute to profitability and growth, or are executives just looking for folks who say yes to everything? There may be many issues affecting the stability of an organization. A business might need to bring in an outside consultant to assist in addressing some of the organization's issues, or a change in leadership may even be in order.

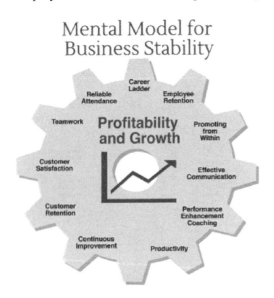

The mindset of how the business is run, the management style, policies, procedures, etc. can very much come out of the environment those in leadership grew up in. Refer again to the mental models of instability, stability, and long-term stability. Are there patterns that are bleeding over into the stability or instability of the business?

Sometimes creating drastic changes in the way people do business can be as simple as changing their expectations. What I am addressing in this book are those issues that impact the business when employers expect the same mindset from every employee—usually a mindset very similar to their own, the mindset of stability. This creates a disconnect when employers don't see the results they expect, especially from employees living in daily instability.

A group of employers in Grand Rapids, Michigan, was experiencing very difficult problems with attendance. Rather than continuing to discipline their employees, they banded together into a resource network for employers. They realized unreliable transportation was a big problem: Not only were people's personal cars unreliable, the lack of city bus lines with good timing to accommodate various shifts made it impossible for most of their employees to achieve perfect attendance. As a result of this collaboration and investigation, the companies created their own van pool that met their specific needs, and attendance became more reliable. This was a multi-company strategy that added to the infrastructure of the community and built resources for employees who wanted to benefit from the van pool.

In a similar stabilizing venture, a manufacturing firm in New Mexico wanted their employees to report for work at 6 a.m., but the local daycare did not open until 6:30 a.m. Stephanie Castillo in human resources was starting to see a trend of employees being late because of childcare issues, so they called the daycare and explained the situation. The daycare executive did some calculations and offered to open at 6 a.m. if the manufacturer could guarantee seven employees would sign up their children. The manufacturing business helped the employees sign up and arranged to deduct the daycare payments from their paychecks and pay the daycare each week. This one action helped stabilize the employees and the employer, and it brought new business to the daycare.

As employers create more stability for the business, they are also building resources for their employees. The investment in the van pool and the arrangement with the daycare provider brought together employers with similar concerns/issues and leveraged those partnerships to end recurring employee problems that were causing problems for the businesses. The investment was much less expensive than continuing to deal with attendance issues and terminating otherwise capable employees. Instead, a minimal investment in a partnership created stability that moved the needle toward profitability and growth.

Business
Perspective

"Helping employees develop themselves professionally creates a more motivated and dedicated workforce. When promoting from within, the learning curve is much shorter, as the individual is already engaged in your workforce and understands the culture of the environment. These same individuals are motivators for new employees because they can see there is a career path within the company."

Employee
Perspective

"Thankfully my bosses are mentors. If not for my bosses who have mentored me, I would've left. I was so scared."

"If I got promoted, I would be in the position of my best friend at work. I don't want to be promoted right now."

CHAPTER 3

Retention and Promoting from Within – Issues and Benefits

Research indicates there are many good reasons to promote from within instead of hiring from outside the firm. For starters, it is more expensive to hire externally. According to the *Wall Street Journal,* a study by Matthew Bidwell at Wharton found that it costs around 18% more to hire from the outside.[35] There is a lot to be said for an employee who already understands the corporate culture and the company-specific skills that are needed in a role. In addition, it takes time and money from a human resources perspective to hire and train an outside candidate. That's the first point: Promoting from within costs less.

Secondly, the existing employee has proven a degree of loyalty to the organization. Bidwell found that 61% of new hires were more likely to be downsized or fired from the position and 21% more likely to leave of their own accord than someone promoted from within.[36]

Thirdly, transitioning to the new role takes less time, and productivity remains at a higher level. The internally promoted employee already has knowledge of the organization's goals, structures, and routines. Unlike internally promoted employees, external hires do not hit the ground running on the first day.

Lastly, an employer already has an established relationship with the internally promoted employee. It can take a long time to develop relationships that work well and establish trust with new employees. An external hire can upset the corporate culture, whereas the internal hire is a proven entity.

Hidden Talent Quadrant Model

There are many reasons to promote from within and many reasons to identify and develop existing talent, including low-wage employees currently living in daily instability. One tool to use in tandem with personality tests is the hidden talent quadrant model. This tool looks at how employees process information based upon the environment in which they were raised. The assessment helps employers better understand the workforce and how they can develop talent within the employee base.

The Hidden Talent Quadrant Model

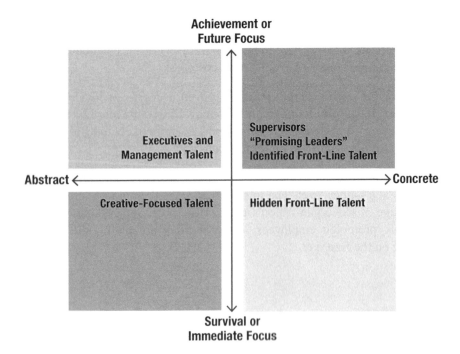

The model uses two main concepts from the environments of instability and stability to create the axes. This chart is able to show relationships among possible attributes of employees.

The vertical axis is about the forces that drive people's mindsets and behaviors. This relates back to the environment in which people were raised, how they spend their time, and what their motivations are.

The horizontal axis is how individuals digest information. It is about how people break down information in their minds and how they arrange and use the information. Individuals who live in daily instability often think very concretely. Abstract thinking is not the dominant form in an unstable environment. When people think concretely, they are dealing with objects and/or events available to the senses. At work this might be the cash register, the forklift, the conveyor belt, the computer scanner, etc.

When people think abstractly, they are dealing with ideas, concepts, and terms used to represent concrete steps or plans. This might take the form of a marketing or strategic plan, an initial public offering, or a profit/loss statement. Abstract thinking is facilitated by the formal register of language. Businesses operate daily from an orientation to the abstract. If an employee has only processed information from a concrete perspective when all information at work is given abstractly, then there will be a huge disconnect.

There are those employees who think concretely and those who think abstractly. Employers need both.

In the model, the horizontal axis representing concrete to abstract runs left to right on a continuum. Those employees who think concretely are most often employees from daily instability. Those who think abstractly are often those who lead the organization, develop the long-range strategy, and negotiate the deals that keep the company at the forefront of the industry.

The vertical axis represents the influence the two different driving forces have in the workplace: stability in a future story at the top, and relative instability at the bottom in survival focus. This information shapes how employees are thinking, living, and where their mindsets are when they are at work. In the top left quadrant of the chart is the correlation between achievement and abstract thinking. This is where the mental models of daily stability and long-term stability are located. In the bottom right is the correlation between concrete thinking and daily survival. This is where the mental model for daily instability is located.

Employees who fall into the top left quadrant are people with highly developed abstract thinking skills and a very strong future focus. These are the employees who make the daily operations decisions and create companywide policies and procedures. They are the business owners, CEOs, executive VPs, and business leaders.

The employees in the top right quadrant are supervisors and front-line talent who have already been tapped for promotions. Business leaders see potential in these people because they have leadership qualities. Leadership has a future story in common with these employees and knows that with more mentoring and coaching on company vision and abstract thinking, they will move up the ladder.

The employees in the lower left quadrant are engineers, trainers, fashion designers, journalists, social media specialists—people who think abstractly while also working to meet tight deadlines with a more immediate focus. They are the creative group who sometimes don't play by the company rule book but contribute a lot to the success of the business. They can be difficult to manage, but we love them, right? Right?

The employees who fall into the bottom right quadrant are often the employees on the front line, the employees who quit or get fired often, the employees who are living in daily instability and appear not to fit in well with the rest of the corporate culture. These are the employees to mentor and promote from within. Employers need to take the extra step with these employees and mentor them based on the resources they bring to the table that can be developed.

The utility of this tool is that when you think of employees, you can see which quadrant they fit into and which quadrants they might fit into with a little help. Managers, leaders, and human resource professionals can use this to mentor an employee into another quadrant based on corporate initiatives. This tool fits nicely with personality tests that may already be in use in the new employee orientation and promotion process.

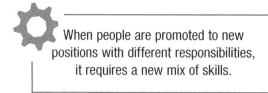

When people are promoted to new positions with different responsibilities, it requires a new mix of skills.

Daily Instability and Retention Issues

Payne's work indicates that some of the retention issues employers will face with entry-level, lower-wage employees from daily instability are:

1. The relative instability of employees' resources: The tyranny of the moment means that employees may have access to a resource one week that dries up the next week. Maybe Grandpa gets sick and can't watch the kids anymore while their mom is at work. A downside of having relationships as a key driving force and resource is that people are unpredictable. Access to resources may change quickly depending on whether or not others can and will cooperate.

2. The hidden rules of time and money: Business leaders' driving force is achievement. They will work long hours to get the job done while keeping an eye on a bonus or the next promotion. If the driving force is relationships, people will treat relationships like an insurance policy and prioritize them over money earned for time spent at work.

3. The role of relationships in daily instability: Since relationships have the greatest impact for people in daily instability, employers must create relationships of mutual respect with all employees, and especially those employees struggling in daily instability. Ensuring that respect flows both ways in these relationships will help get employers the productivity they are looking for.

   Stephanie Castillo, human resources executive, says, "I build relationships with the entry-level employees at our manufacturing firm. I try to understand where they are in their lives and where I might help them achieve more stability."[37]

   In fact, the top factor for employee engagement is relationships with coworkers, as noted in one employee job satisfaction and engagement survey. The second most important factor? The opportunity to use your skills and abilities, followed by the relationship with your immediate supervisor.

4. The acquired knowledge bases for work: The environment people grew up in determines to a large extent the knowledge base they will bring to work. Compare the experiences of an employee with two college-educated parents to an employee whose family has lived in daily instability for two generations. Each employee will bring a different knowledge base to work that was shaped by the particular environment.

Daily Instability and Promotion Issues

There can be obstacles to promoting individuals from daily instability. These issues include:

1. The loss of relationships: To move out of daily instability one may need to give up relationships or modify relationships for achievement (at least for a period of time). This is hard for people who rely on relationships as their safety net or insurance policy. Dr. Payne says that there are four reasons a person will work to leave instability: It is too painful to stay, they have a vision or a goal, they have a key relationship with someone outside instability, or they have a special talent or skill.

2. Change in identity: Comparing the hidden rules of daily instability with those in daily stability reveals many ways in which social inclusion, relationships, love, and acceptance are driving forces for those in daily instability. But a change in identity like a promotion may change relationships, and not necessarily for the better. If you ride the bus every day with your best friend from work, and then she gets promoted and becomes your supervisor, your friendship might change. For instance, your friend might stop riding the bus and buy a car. In the neighborhood they might say she got "too big for her britches" or "above her raisins." When employers anticipate that it will be an issue, they can put some mentoring measures into place to deal with it.

   Sonia told me one of the best things her employer did for her was to hold her accountable to policies, procedures, and company standards. She was treated just like an employee from stability but with the understanding that, as she put it, "I needed room for learning and adjusting not just to my job duties but to every aspect of my life."

3. Moving from an hourly wage position to a beginning supervision position is a big jump because of the additional resource base that is needed. Written and verbal language and communication skills, planning, abstract thinking, and analysis of detail are all required.

LeLinda, recently promoted into a supervisory role, said her new position requires more paperwork, more team management responsibilities, and management of a secretary. She has to be intentional about being more organized and structured with her time.

4. The extent of organizational resources: The relative stability or instability of resources within a business can greatly affect what can be offered to an employee. On-the-job training, paid time off, a 401(k), education benefits, and fitness programs all add to the stability of an employee. This discussion is about the resources and benefits available at the company.

5. Organizational demands change at different levels: An employee moving into a new position might not understand the demands of that position and may need some coaching. This new position will almost certainly require additional skill sets, as LeLinda witnessed in her promotion.

Even though there can be retention and promotion issues, it is still worth the time to retain employees and promote them from within. Considering the cost of replacing an employee and the benefits of promoting from within, employers get better return on investment than they would with new hires.

Knowing there will be issues allows employers to design internal systems to compensate for them.

Business
Perspective

*"If you dress sloppily as an employee,
then I make a judgment about you."*

*"The hidden rules really hit us. We had not given
thought to why employees do what they do."*

Employee
Perspective

*"Before Getting Ahead, all my rules were from how I was
raised, and my attitude was 'take me as I am.' Now I'm open to
learning and understanding the hidden rules of middle class.
I need to learn the norm to be the norm."*

*"I go to work, but nobody told me the hidden rules
of the business. Knowing what they want and
what they say are two different things."*

CHAPTER 4

Hidden Rules in the Workplace

A hidden rule is an unspoken cue or habit of a group. People bring to work the hidden rules with which they were raised; these hidden rules often arise from the economic environment in which an employee lives.

Hidden rules were first defined by Ruby Payne in her book *A Framework for Understanding Poverty.* Since then the concept has been widely applied in many sectors, including business.

In a given situation, if people know the hidden rules, they are in good shape and don't have to explain themselves. If they break a hidden rule, however, people look at them like they are stupid or obvious outsiders. It's important to note that one set of hidden rules is not better than another. Quite the opposite: The more rules people know, the more successful they can be. The knowledge of hidden rules leads to access, and access leads to power. Knowing the hidden rules of the group helps in navigating unfamiliar and difficult situations.

At work, knowing the hidden rules allows us to create more effective policies and procedures by understanding the behaviors of the employees and business partners. Employers can use these hidden rules to build relationships, reduce workplace conflict, and build the resources of employees.

Some hidden rules are easily broken, but if people are intuitive, they can navigate unfamiliar and difficult situations better because of their knowledge of the rules. When employers know the hidden rules, they can create relationships of mutual respect based on their understanding of the rules of different groups—in this case employees, coworkers, the customer base, and investors.

At one point in my career, I was a regional manager of three college bookstores. Darin worked for me in shipping and receiving and was a great worker. He lived in a mobile home park and took public transportation to and from work. One day there was a stabbing on the city bus, and at work we were discussing how this happened. Darin shared that he carried a switchblade in his boot for safety. On one hand I was alarmed to discover I had an employee who had a switchblade on him. On the other hand, I knew that because of where he lived and his transportation options, he was juggling the concerns of two different worlds. The blade was what he needed for his world of daily instability, but in order to maintain the stable environment of the workplace, I needed him to leave it at home. I told him if I ever saw signs of the knife at work, he would be dismissed. I'm proud to say that Darin was quick to learn the hidden rules of daily stability and adapted as needed. He is now a manager and supervisor of others.

Renee, a Getting Ahead graduate, told me that years ago she worked as a cook in a restaurant, but she wanted to be a cashier. Even though she expressed her interest to the manager multiple times, she was never moved into the cashier position, and the manager never gave her a good reason why. Renee observed that the people the manager hired for that role all dressed and talked a certain way. She changed how she dressed, how she wore her hair, and most importantly, she changed how she talked to her manager. In a matter of weeks she was hired into the front-of-house position. Because the manager could not articulate his expectations for the position, Renee's observation helped her figure out the hidden rules that were in play.

Every business has hidden rules. Part of my onboarding with new employees when I was president of aha! Process was to tell them the top hidden rules of the company. It allowed them to be more successful right out of the gate without stumbling over too many hidden rules—as I had! Now when I consult with a new company, I always ask what the most important hidden rules are. I suggest these rules be added to the employee handbook and onboarding process so they aren't so hidden anymore.

Once, a week after I had started a new executive-level position, another vice president at my new firm called me. I could tell I was getting chewed out, but I didn't know why. I finally asked what I had done. In that person's view, I had not followed the protocol for asking a question. I had broken a hidden rule of the company, and the other executive made me feel ashamed. I have never forgotten that. I also had a boss whose hidden rule was that if the meeting started at 8 a.m., employees should arrive no later than 7:50. It was an unspoken rule that if someone arrived later, they were considered tardy or unprepared.

The problem with hidden rules is that they are often used to blame and shame people who don't follow them. Employees are no exception. People don't all have common experiences to draw from within the workforce, and so there are differences that people must contend with. For everyone in a company to be successful, people need to learn their rules and teach their rules to each other—especially the hidden rules. If people don't understand each other's hidden rules, this is where unconscious bias and prejudice can start creeping in. Once people recognize the hidden rules, they can begin talking about issues and actions in a nonjudgmental way.

Consider asking new hires after six weeks what is different at your company that they haven't seen at other companies. What rules have they observed or had to learn that no one told them about? Some people don't intuit the hidden rules, and they often look like hiring mistakes; however, they may not be. They may simply need to be taught the hidden rules of the business.

Hidden Rules Among Classes[38]

	DAILY INSTABILITY
POSSESSIONS	People
MONEY	To be used, spent
PERSONALITY	Is for entertainment; sense of humor is highly valued
SOCIAL EMPHASIS	Social inclusion of people who are liked
FOOD	Key question: Did you have enough? Quantity important
CLOTHING	Valued for individual style and expression of personality
TIME	Present most important; decisions made for the moment based on feelings or survival
EDUCATION	Valued and revered as abstract but not as reality
DESTINY	Believes in fate; cannot do much to mitigate chance
LANGUAGE	Casual register; language is about survival
FAMILY STRUCTURE	Tends to be matriarchal
WORLDVIEW	Sees world in terms of local setting
LOVE	Love and acceptance conditional, based on whether individual is liked
DRIVING FORCES	Survival, relationships, entertainment
HUMOR	About people and sex

DAILY STABILITY	LONG-TERM STABILITY
Things	One-of-a-kind objects, legacies, pedigrees
To be managed	To be conserved, invested
Is for acquisition and stability; achievement is highly valued	Is for connections; financial, political, social connections are highly valued
Emphasis is on self-governance and self-sufficiency	Emphasis is on social exclusion
Key question: Did you like it? Quality important	Key question: Was it presented well? Presentation important
Valued for its quality and acceptance into norm of middle class; label important	Valued for its artistic sense and expression; designer important
Future most important; decisions made against future ramifications	Traditions and history most important; decisions made partially on basis of tradition and decorum
Crucial for climbing success ladder and making money	Necessary tradition for making and maintaining connections
Believes in choice; can change future with good choices now	*Noblesse oblige*
Formal register; language is about negotiation	Formal register; language is about networking
Tends to be patriarchal	Depends on who has the money
Sees world in terms of national setting	Sees world in terms of international view
Love and acceptance conditional and based largely on achievement	Love and acceptance conditional and related to social standing and connections
Work, achievement	Financial, political, social connections
About situations	About social *faux pas*

Considering Economic Class Diversity Builds Stability for All: A Conversation with Fred Keller

Fred Keller is CEO and owner of Cascade Engineering, a manufacturer serving the automotive, commercial truck and bus, solid waste and recycling, furniture, and material handling industries.

Cascade Engineering is a global company with 1,600 employees located in 14 facilities throughout North America and additional facilities in Budapest, Hungary. As one of the largest certified B Corporations in the world, Cascade Engineering is a nationally recognized proponent of sustainable business practices that emphasize the key role business can play in building financial, social, and environmental capital.

Fred, you deserve the credit for embedding economic diversity considerations more deeply within business. What was behind this for you?

The important thing I wanted to figure out was how to have a business answering the needs of all people as opposed to being very selective. I started out with the idea of being supportive of all folks and trying to make it work for them, including a welfare-to-career program. That has been my desire as a child of the '60s: trying to figure it all out and make a business that is more humane than what I experienced when I was working for a very large corporation with 60,000 employees. I wanted to develop something that was workable for all folks.

You had some unsuccessful attempts at a welfare-to-career program before you had success. What actions finally made it work?

Our story goes back to a couple of attempts to figure this out. How could we hire folks into CE [Cascade Engineering] and help them be successful in our environment? Ron Jimmerson, a machine operator in the factory, was the first one I talked to about this. He had a social work background and helped organize a van that we used daily to pick up homeless people and bring them into our

(continued on next page)

A Conversation with Fred Keller (continued)

employment and put them to work. Everyone was all smiles, and within six weeks, all gone. It didn't work for us. We scratched our heads and said, "Well, that didn't work." Ron and I were both chagrined about the situation.

A year or two later, CE partnered with a fast food operator/owner, the Department of Social Services, nonprofits, and other agencies to support employees. The fast food operator/owner suggested that he train employees up and have them work for him for six months with the promise that after six months they could transfer into a higher-paying job, which was actually a position with CE.

Around that same time, I was introduced to Phil DeVol from aha! Process, and he introduced us to Ruby Payne's work. We started putting the economic class thought process into it and came to understand we have people who haven't had work experience, and now we add in the cultural experience that is different.

We started working on three things simultaneously: One, the idea of agencies and nonprofits supporting us. We put a social worker from the state on our factory floor to support our folks. Two, inclusion and training on the critical element of understanding what it means to be in poverty. And three, we added pay for contribution depending not on how long you were on the job but on what you had learned.

We want our employees at Cascade to have a career with us, to stay until retirement, to provide visibility, and to have a level of potential within the organization.

What changed for Cascade when all the forces came together?

We didn't change our expectations or our work rules. It was important for our organization not to change that. Our methodology was to be supportive of those who were having difficulties so they could achieve just like anyone else can achieve. If you treat those in the welfare-to-career program differently or have lower expectations,

(continued on next page)

A Conversation with Fred Keller (continued)

they don't feel good about it, we don't feel good about it, and coworkers don't feel good about it. It is important to have the same expectations of achievement for everyone. We found that there is no problem in achievement as long as they are supported.

We of course did implement some changes and do business differently. We implemented a buddy system where everyone was assigned to someone in the organization who was experienced to help and guide.

We improved our onboarding and orientation process so it was more uniform, and everyone going through had an understanding of the whole process and what is expected of them. We improved our human resources management because we saw good reason for doing it and supporting those folks in the welfare-to-career program at the same time.

Of course, having Joyce, the caseworker, on the factory floor was just magic and a key point. And we were developing our pay-for-contribution program. We were very much learning what it meant to have expectations for our employees. Often entry-level jobs are dead-end jobs, and we were determined to demonstrate to ourselves that if people were learning more and contributing more to the organization, we could pay them more. Pay for contribution was our effort to make that happen.

What is the best return on investment for you with this program?

The best return is the knowledge that people are able to enter our organization knowing that they are going to be accepted and supported and knowing that they are valued. Having a system of support in the organization where people know they want to work there because of who the organization is and what the organization is, that's so much more rewarding than the idea that they are working there in order to get money to get somewhere else. I believe it is borne out in the culture: Employees genuinely feel safer at work than in life at home or in the community. They feel like it is a place they enjoy being as opposed to a place where they go to make money. That to me is the return on investment.

Thank you to Fred and Cascade Engineering for beginning the thinking about stability from an economic class perspective. This, in turn, has led to years of continuous improvement, innovation, and risk undertaken by hundreds of businesses all seeking to stabilize their workplaces and employees, creating what we know generically today as resource networks for employers.

How can employers apply knowledge of the hidden rules of daily instability in the workplace to create relationships that motivate employees to achieve the productivity employers seek? Take a look at the attitudes and behaviors below that build relationships versus attitudes and behaviors that destroy potential relationships with employees.

 Constructive Attitudes and Behaviors

 Destructive Attitudes and Behaviors

Constructive Attitudes and Behaviors	Destructive Attitudes and Behaviors
Seek first to understand	Assuming you know what the employee thinks and feels
Appreciate employee's humor	Putdowns or sarcasm about the employee's humor
Accept what the employee cannot say about a person or situation (loyalty to the absent)	Demands for full explanation
Respect the demands and priorities of relationships	Insistence that achievement supersedes relationships
Use the adult voice	Using the parent voice
Assist with goal setting	Telling the employee his/her goals
Identify options related to available resources	Making judgments on value and availability of resources

It takes time to build relationships of mutual respect. When employers do, they reap the rewards of loyalty, productivity, and having employees who are engaged.

Business Perspective

"I tell my team, 'I need you to speak professionally, like the people on the television news.'"

"We spend a lot of time on language with new hires to get what we want for our customer service."

Employee Perspective

"I learned I had the ability to code-switch between casual and formal language. Code-switching and other resources provided me the means to get out of poverty and stay out."

"You speak like a hillbilly, and you will be treated like a hillbilly. Now I think before I speak. There are smart people in poverty who simply can't explain themselves."

The Language of Business

Like the hidden rules people bring with them to work, language, word choices, grammar, and communication styles are also influenced by the environment in which people were raised. People's ability in their first or even second language can affect their understanding of directions, manuals, instructions, and even social interactions at work. Employers who better understand the environment of daily instability can use that understanding to gain insight into challenges that occur in the workplace because of communication and language barriers. Now let's explore five aspects of language that can impact a company's success.

Of U.S. adults more than 16 years of age, 14% read at or below a fifth-grade reading level, 29% read at the eighth-grade level, and 43% live in poverty.[39] When employees have low literacy skills, the result is a lack of performance on the job. This means trouble for the employer.

Many employers find that they must upgrade the skill sets of the team members to get the work process and flow that they are striving for. In fact, 50% of Fortune 500 companies spend $300 million per year on basic skills training, including literacy.[40]

In the book *Meaningful Differences in the Everyday Experience of Young American Children,* researchers Hart and Risley show that children ages 1–4 in professional households are exposed to more words than children ages 1–4 in welfare households. (The word *welfare* is the word used in Hart and Risley's book.) In this same book, Hart and Risley found that there was one affirmation for every two prohibitions in welfare homes, two affirmations for every prohibition in working class homes, and six affirmations for every prohibition in professional families.[41] Consider a child who jumps up on the couch to look out the window at a bird. In a home in daily stability, a parent will likely engage the child and, using lots of words, find out what's out the window. In a home in daily instability, there is a high probability you will hear only two words: "Get down."

Many times an affirmation in a professional home is also followed with the "what" and "why" of a situation, with elaboration meant to expand thinking. People in daily stability rarely just talk about the bird with their kids; they talk about the red bird, which is a cardinal, and the cardinal is the state bird of Ohio. They might go on to tell the child what the bird eats, where it lives, and when the child is most likely to see one. Similarly, when people from daily stability give a prohibition, they usually follow it up with an explanation, the what and why. Instead of telling a child simply to get down, people from daily stability will usually explain why it isn't a good idea to jump on the couch and the potential consequences of falling off the couch, for example.

LeLinda, a youth guidance specialist supervisor at her workplace, told me one positive outcome of her participation in the Getting Ahead curriculum is that now she examines cause and effect not only with her children but with her employees and clients as well. Because of this one change, her relationships have improved, and she's seen a boost in the productivity of the people she manages.

When employees have difficulty reading, which results in the inability to complete forms, follow directions, read technology manuals, etc., it creates an embarrassment that isolates the employees from other social developments happening in the workplace and in the community. On the other hand, improvements in literacy have been correlated with enhancements in self-esteem. When employees have higher self-esteem, they contribute at a higher level.[42]

In fact, when employees have been able to improve their literacy skills, businesses report these results:[43]

Skills Gained by Employees	Percent of Employers
Greater willingness and ability to learn for life	85
Improved ability to listen, to understand, and to learn and apply information	84
More positive attitude toward change	84
Better ability to build and work in teams	80
Increased understanding of and ability to use numbers by themselves or in charts and tables	76
Improved capacity to think critically and act logically to evaluate situations, solve problems, and make decisions	73

The improvements benefit the business as well:[44]

Benefits to Employers	Percent of Employers
Improved employee morale/self-esteem	87
Increased quality of work	82
Improved capacity to solve problems	82
Better team performance	82
Improved capacity to cope with change in the workplace	75
Improved capacity to use new technology	73
More employees participating in job-specific training	73

Clearly it's not impossible for adults with low literacy to gain new language skills. The point for leadership is that some employees in the workplace may have far less language experience than other employees. Employers can provide training to improve literacy skills, and there are implications for many aspects of the workplace: The employee manual, onboarding, instructions for learning processes, communication with the customer base, and more may need to be retailored to the language ability employees bring to the table.

Concrete vs. Abstract

Many employees coming from two or more generations of daily instability will use and respond best to concrete language. If there are differences in the workplace where it looks like people are talking the same language but the way they process it is different, this may be a concrete vs. abstract information processing issue. If so, changes to new-employee onboarding, discipline policies, conflict resolution procedures, explanation of the benefits package, etc. may help avoid misunderstandings. While employers can benefit from adopting the concrete language of their employees from daily instability, they should also remember to model abstract speech so employees develop the ability to use both. Like knowing and using various hidden rules, knowing and using different modes of speech can be a valuable resource.

If low-wage employees have lived in daily instability for multiple generations, there is a good chance they won't understand the meanings of some abstract words. If they don't understand the meanings, then they can't follow the directions. In the interviews I had with Getting Ahead graduates, language was almost always at the top of the list as a barrier to their business success.

This means that to be successful, in addition to keeping their words concrete, employers should use more mental models (pictures, stories, and analogies), video clips, and infographics to engage and communicate with employees. Why? All of these modes of communication appeal to the senses of those that struggle with abstract language and thoughts. As a leader, it is your responsibility to deliver information to employees in a way that is easily understood so that company initiatives can be implemented correctly to meet goals quickly.

Michelle Wood, who was inspired to go to college after completing Getting Ahead, told me that when she was in class, she would write down the words she didn't understand. On Fridays, while she was at the Laundromat, she would look up the words in a dictionary and begin using them in her everyday speech. She said her friends would "call her out" for using words too big for her. But what Michelle realized was that to be successful in work and school, she had to talk like her managers and her professors.

Registers of Language

Dutch linguist Martin Joos found people can go one register down in a conversation and be accepted. However, to drop two registers in a conversation is socially offensive.

REGISTER	EXPLANATION
FROZEN	Language that is always the same. For example: Lord's Prayer, wedding vows, etc.
FORMAL	The standard sentence syntax and word choice of work and school. Has complete sentences and specific word choice.
CONSULTATIVE	Formal register when used in conversation. Discourse pattern not quite as direct as formal register.
CASUAL	Language between friends characterized by a 400- to 800-word vocabulary. Word choice general and not specific. Conversation dependent upon nonverbal assists. Sentence syntax often incomplete.
INTIMATE	Language between lovers or twins. Language of sexual harassment.

Sources: Joos, M. (1967). The styles of the five clocks. In R. D. Abraham & R. C. Troike (Eds.), *Language and cultural diversity in American education* (pp. 145–149).
Payne, R. K., DeVol, P. E., & Dreussi-Smith, T. (2009). *Bridges out of poverty: Strategies for professionals and communities* (4th rev. ed.).

Formal register is required in most workplaces, especially if the job involves writing reports, emails, etc. Formal register has a 1,200- to 1,600-word working vocabulary. Consultative register, which is also used at work, is a mix of formal and casual register that tends to be more spoken. Abstract words make up a large part of the formal register vocabulary, and business leaders use abstract words and phrases all the time: *onboarding, strategic plan, marketing plan, OSHA, HIPAA,* and *time management* are a few examples.

Casual register, on the other hand, is language commonly used between friends. It comes out of the oral language tradition of any group of people and has about a 400- to 800-word working vocabulary. Maria Montano-Harmon, a linguist in California, found that in daily instability virtually all that the adults know is casual register.[45]

How does this affect productivity, performance, and customer service at work? If people don't know what a word means, they can't act upon it. People can't understand directions or tasks if they are missing key pieces of the vocabulary used to communicate those directions or tasks. Thus it is important that manuals, directions, and tasks use casual, concrete language when possible. Business leaders can use pictures, video clips, maps, infographics, comic strips, or other visual aids to help maximize efficiency. The more employers can lead with visuals, the better their engagement will be. When businesses can model their intentions with their employees, they get better outcomes.

I was on a business trip and ended up in a small café by the hotel for a late lunch. The server approached the table and said abruptly, "We ain't got any of the daily special left." If I were her employer, I might advise her that her tips would improve if she said something a little more formal, like, "Good afternoon. I just wanted to let you know that we are out of the daily special, but I can recommend the turkey sandwich. It is one of the most requested items on the menu." Exploring the use of casual and formal register within the workplace makes business dollars and cents.

Casual-register language is at the root of some physical conflicts in the workplace. Formal register is the language of conflict resolution and negotiation, and many times employees from daily instability will not have the words to resolve a conflict. As a result, conflicts often escalate into violence. Tempers are lost, and pushing, shoving, and yelling obscenities are common signs that communication has broken down and a fight is brewing. Most conflict resolution experts say that to resolve a conflict, people have to get away from the personal and focus on the issue. But in order to address issues, most times people need abstract, formal-register words.

Story Structure and Discourse Patterns – Formal vs. Casual

When someone tells a story in formal register, it is usually very direct in nature and progresses chronologically from beginning to middle to end. When a story is told in casual register, it tends to be circular in nature and involves lots of nonverbals and coworker participation. Employees from daily instability not only use mostly casual register, how they tell stories is different as well. How they answer supervisors' questions can also be different and at times frustrating.

The formal story structure is expected at work as well as in other settings where formal register is the norm. The formal story structure has a clear beginning, middle, and end. It gets to the point. Employers expect employees to use the formal story structure and register when explaining why they are late for work or why something at work isn't working properly. Employers don't want to hear a circular story that relies heavily on nonverbals.

The casual story structure is entertaining. The story may begin at the end instead of what people in stability might consider the beginning. The employee may include unrelated but informative details about coworkers, workflow, or policies and procedures that are not working. The story might include lots of background information that may be more confusing than helpful. It might also contain what people from daily stability would consider too much personal information. A manager might get frustrated with the casual story structure because the employee is not getting to the point quickly enough for the manager's schedule.

**Formal-Register
Discourse Pattern**

**Casual-Register
Discourse Pattern**

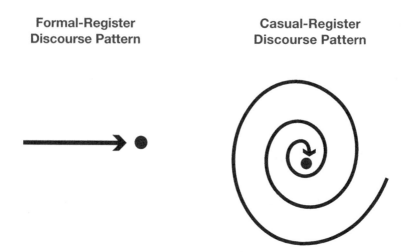

Employers certainly expect that formal register will be used when employees interact with customers, but the best case is an employee who is able to use both patterns. Formal discourse patterns are about getting down to business, while casual discourse is about reestablishing relationships *before* people get down to business.

Renee, an emergency relief manager who grew up in daily instability, encountered a woman who said she "talked the same at work as she talks with her friends," but it wasn't working out so well for her. The woman had recently been fired for arguing with a customer. In contrast, many of the Getting Ahead graduates I talked to, including Renee, had a well-developed ability to code-switch when needed. They were able to speak the language of the environment they were in.

Getting Ahead graduate and inventory specialist Jesse Quintana told me that after he was exposed to this information about story structure, he was able to understand how to approach different members of management. One manager was straightforward and didn't want to hear any circular stories. Jesse would give information to that manager in a very straightforward and unemotional manner. Another manager liked input and ideas and enjoyed hearing stories that broadened the conversation. Jesse learned when and how to code-switch based on which manager he was talking with.

Do employers make expectations for formal register explicit with employees, and do they offer training and tools to help employees meet those expectations? Or is the formal register requirement a hidden rule that sometimes leads to misunderstandings?

When an employee answers with a circular story structure, enjoy the story—it is intended to create connection, to strengthen relationships, and to be entertaining. Then, as a manager, pull out the facts you wanted and expected to hear from what you were told, and run them back by the employee for verification: "Now, let me get this clear. You're telling me that … " You should get to a "yes" as you repeat the distilled version, but if you got something wrong, the employee should jump in to correct you, since no one likes to feel they've been misunderstood. If leadership makes this a standard practice, employees will learn how to answer questions more directly.

Joyce, a state caseworker supporting employees at a manufacturing plant in Michigan, says she just wants her clients to get to the point. "Just cut to the chase and tell me your problem," she used to say, but she has learned both to have patience and to teach her clients how to be more direct in their communication. She told me, "I tell them respectfully, 'We will get back to that one; right now we need to concentrate on this subject.'"

According to David Sibbet, author of *Visual Leaders,* people make sense of spoken language in four ways:

1. The sequence in the sentence: the subject, verb, modifier, etc.

2. Definition: the official dictionary definition, as well as the slang meaning(s) of a word, if any.

3. Connotation: an idea or quality a word brings to mind in addition to its meaning.

4. Expression: the emphasis on spoken words and the sounds that express emotion while talking.[46]

Sibbet argues that "to compare different ideas and information, you have to make a display somewhere. Since humans don't live only in linear time, and stories occur in contexts and environments, verbal language depends on words pointing at images we can imagine as it goes along. The listener creates the pictures in his or her own imagination."[47] Leaders are more effective when they provide concrete-thinking employees the tools needed to interpret spoken language from leadership.

Voices

Eric Berne, a therapist who created transactional analysis, says there are three voices: a parent voice, an adult voice, and a child voice.[48] The child voice is petulant and self-interested. The parent voice is authoritative and gives firm directives. The adult voice is the voice of reason and compromise. When these voices are internalized as self-talk, they play back like recorded messages from childhood—sometimes put there by others, sometimes messages people have created for themselves. These inner voices reflect people's concept of what they were taught, of relationships, of how life feels, and of how people think about the world.

THE CHILD VOICE

*Defensive, victimized, emotional, whining,
losing attitude, strongly negative nonverbals*

- Quit picking on me.
- You don't love me.
- You want me to leave.
- Nobody likes (loves) me.
- I hate you.
- You're ugly.

- You make me sick.
- It's your fault.
- Don't blame me.
- She, he, _____ did it.
- You make me mad.
- You made me do it.

THE PARENT VOICE

Authoritative, directive, judgmental, evaluative, win-lose mentality, demanding, punitive, sometimes threatening

- You shouldn't (should) do that.
- It's wrong (right) to do _____.
- That's stupid, immature, out of line, ridiculous.
- Life's not fair. Get busy.
- You do as I say.
- If you weren't so _____, this wouldn't happen to you.
- Why can't you be like _____?

THE ADULT VOICE

Nonjudgmental, free of negative nonverbals, factual, often in question format, attitude of win-win

- In what ways could this be resolved?
- What factors will be used to determine the effectiveness, quality of _____?
- I would like to recommend _____.
- What are choices in this situation?
- I am comfortable (uncomfortable) with _____.
- Options that could be considered are _____.
- For me to be comfortable, I need the following things to occur: _____.
- These are the consequences of that choice/action: _____.
- We agree to disagree.

The "inner parent voice" is ingrained in people by their parents, teachers, and caregivers. It reflects the concepts of life they were taught. The parent voice is made up of many messages that come out in phrases like:

"You shouldn't (should) do that. It's wrong (right) to do _____."

The nonverbal communication and body language that goes with the parent voice is often angry, with impatient gestures, finger pointing, and a loud voice. The phrases used tend to be dictatorial, authoritative, directive, judgmental, evaluative, demanding, punitive, and threatening.

Have you ever had a manager who used the parent voice? I have. It felt like one of my former bosses had *only* the parent voice! Like a stern parent, she kept employees fearful of admonishment. After a while, however, she became ineffective at managing by fear because she lost respect from her direct reports. As her employee I felt more like the manager in some of the heated conversations because I was the one controlling the conversation and keeping it in the adult voice.

The "inner child voice" is reactionary and represents people's immediate response to what they see, feel, and hear from the world around them. When people are angry or afraid, the child voice can dominate self-talk and therefore thinking; the child is in control. The child voice expresses itself in phrases like: "It's your fault. Don't blame me."

The nonverbal communication and body language that often accompany the child voice can be rolling eyes, shrugging shoulders, temper tantrums, and a whining voice. Phrases tend to be defensive, victimized, emotional, and dictatorial.

You may be thinking, "I'm an adult. I don't use a child's voice." The child voice can still come out in how people communicate with themselves and others even though they are adults now. When people use the child voice in their self-talk, they are usually avoiding responsibility for their own situation. When people use the child voice on others, it can invite the parent voice in response. The child voice can be very manipulative and thus very powerful, but it becomes annoying and tiring to others and eventually harms relationships.

I once had a marketing assistant who had a great child voice when she missed a deadline. A computer glitch was always at fault, and she never failed to place the blame in a whiny voice designed to make her seem helpless when in reality it was her lack of time management skills that was to blame.

As people get older and wiser—with a few successful and failed negotiations under their belts—they develop the ability to slow down and consider their behaviors and actions before they act and talk. The adult voice provides a way to control the parent and child voices. The adult voice is needed for learning and for cooperation. It is used to discover how other people think and feel without upsetting them in the process. The adult voice resolves conflicts. The adult voice can be heard in phrases like:

"I would like to recommend _____. Options that could be considered are _____."

The nonverbal communication and body language that goes with the adult voice is attentive, leaning forward, not threatened or threatening—and the voice is calm. The phrases tend to be respectful, comparative, informative, and reasoned. Questions might include: What, when, where, why, who, how?

Employees who have been in daily instability for two generations or more may use only the parent and child voices; negotiation using the adult voice is neither valued nor effective in daily instability. Leaders and managers, however, should model the adult voice at all times. Maintaining the adult voice pulls the conversation up a level and encourages employees to use the adult voice as well. Employees occasionally will need to hear the parent voice to stop undesirable behavior, but the voice that is best to negotiate and communicate with employees is the adult voice.

Nonverbal Communication and Body Language

A major component of communication, especially for someone skilled in the casual register, is nonverbal communication—the speaker's and the listener's. Without the words to express an emotion or concept, people will turn to nonverbal means of communication like body language and tone of voice. Nonverbal communication is important for everyone in the workplace, not just employees from daily instability, but employers should be especially aware of nonverbal messaging with those employees who are most sensitive to it.

When an employee repeatedly misses deadlines or never shows up to work on time, what emotion does this raise for you? If that's something that pushes your buttons, you might be irritated or even angry. To improve your nonverbal communication, especially with those coming from daily instability, be very aware of your intent. Is your intent to communicate anger? It might make you feel better, but that does not resolve the situation. If your intent is to gain an understanding of what's going on inside or outside of work that is interfering with projects or tasks, be sure you don't give off nonverbal signals that express your anger. These signals can be especially confusing if you are simultaneously using the adult voice.

Managers and leaders can be more attentive to communication style while they listen for the hidden rules in play and what internal or external resources might be needed. If the goals are employee retention and productivity, leadership wants to work with employees to make sure all the resources are in place to get the job done.

Business
Perspective

*"The work we did on future stories was amazing.
The result of this time spent together is that we are
seeing advancement at work and in the home life."*

*"Resources—this is a complex one. There is no doubt
that folks who live in daily instability are every bit
as interesting, resourceful, and thoughtful as you
would expect at any level."*

Employee
Perspective

*"I'm building up my resources so I can move up.
It's no longer cool to be complacent."*

*"I was drinking and using drugs. Instead of needing a job
to drink and use, I looked at what I wanted to do in life,
I changed my life, and I built my resources to get there."*

CHAPTER 6

The Resources of the Employee Base

People living in daily instability are affected by more than just financial resources, and people from daily stability and long-term stability alike have differing access to resources. Resources fall into 11 categories: financial, emotional, mental, spiritual, physical, social capital/ support systems, relationships/role models, knowledge of hidden rules, language/formal register, integrity and trust, and motivation/persistence. The more resources people have, the more potential they have to be successful in life. On the other hand, a high level of one resource doesn't always bring other resources. A person can be financially stable but have low emotional and physical resources, for example. The ability to raise our stability has more to do with the other resources than it does with financial resources alone. Let's look more closely at all 11 resources.

Eleven Resources

1. **Financial** Money to purchase goods/services

2. **Emotional** Ability to control emotional responses

3. **Mental/Cognitive** Mental capability to deal with daily life

4. **Languge/Formal Register** Ability to use appropriate vocabulary and grammar

5. **Social Capital/Support Systems** Friends, family, and other resources to help

6. **Physical** Physical health/mobility

(continued on next page)

Employee Resource Continuum[49]

	0	1
Integrity and Trust	Predictably amoral. Destructive to others. Practices deception.	Inconsistent. Unpredictable. No internal compass. Right and wrong are gray areas.
Financial	Bills unpaid. Creditors calling.	Paycheck to paycheck. Bills paid late.
Emotional	No emotional stamina. Impulsive. Engages in self-destructive behavior (addiction, violence, abusive adult relationships, casual sex).	Moves between voices of child and parent. Blames and accuses. Impulsive mood swings.

Adapted from Krabill/Payne Resource Quotient

7. **Spiritual** Belief in divine purpose/guidance

8. **Integrity/Trust** Trust, predictability, and safety

9. **Motivation and Persistence** Energy, drive, and planning

10. **Relationships/Role Models** Access to people who consistently behave appropriately and are nuturing

11. **Knowledge of Hidden Rules** Know unspoken cues/behaviors of different groups

Adapted from the work of Ruby Payne and Phil DeVol

The resources of employees cause ripple effects across the entire spectrum of business success: Productivity, motivation, work ethic, and stability are all affected by the resources the employee base can access.

2	3	4
Consistently moral, ethical, and legal. Decides in best interests of self. Rationalizes poor decisions.	Decisions are moral, ethical, and legal. Avoids difficult issues. Is responsible for self but blames others.	Decisions are moral, ethical, and legal. Tough issues are addressed. Accepts responsibility for self and is accountable to others.
More income than bills. Some savings.	Building assets in home. Limited investments.	Has net worth other than home. Many investments.
Uses adult voice except in conflict. Outbursts of anger. Sometimes engages in impulsive behavior.	Uses adult voice in conflict. Avoids conflict. Rarely impulsive.	Uses adult voice in conflict. Confronts, yet maintains relationships. Is not impulsive.

(continued on next page)

Employee Resource Continuum (continued)

	0	1
Mental	Relies totally on casual register and nonverbal data to communicate. Not much formal education. Disorganized.	Can read and write formal register. Prefers casual register. Can do basic math. Has difficulty managing time and tasks.
Spiritual Destiny	Has no hope. Believes in fate. Choice and consequence are not linked. Discipline is about punishment, penance, and forgiveness.	Believes in good and bad luck. Few choices are considered. Tries not to get caught.
Physical	Cannot take care of physical self. Requires assistance. Risky behaviors create health problems.	Can take care of self. Or can take care of self but does not. Often sick. Unkempt.
Support System	Alone.	Is providing support for limited group of people, which could include friends or family. Tries to build intimacy at work.
Relationships	Uncommitted relationships that are destructive or damaging.	Few bonding relationships of any kind. Perceives self as unlovable.

Adapted from Krabill/Payne Resource Quotient

2	3	4
Knows when to use formal register. Has some training beyond high school. Can implement a plan if told how. Knows the **what** but not the **how.**	Uses formal register well. Formal education. Can do long-range planning. Knows the **what** and the **how.**	Consistently uses formal register well. Knows the **what** and the **why.** Initiates and executes plans. Congruence between nonverbals and words.
Has no hope. Believes in fate. Choice and consequence are not linked. Discipline is about punishment, penance, and forgiveness.	Believes in good and bad luck. Few choices are considered. Tries not to get caught.	Believes that choices affect destiny. Options are examined. Choices and consequences are linked. Believes in a higher power.
Clean, presentable. Able to take care of self. Mostly healthy.	Attractive. Physically able. Mostly healthy.	Very attractive. Weight, height proportional. Excellent physical health.
Has support system of friends and family. Friends and family may not know appropriate hidden rules of individual's position.	Has support system at work and at home. Knows how to seek help if needed. Friends and family know appropriate hidden rules of individual's position.	Has support system at home, at work, and in community. Has large network of professional colleagues. Can purchase help if needed.
Several personal relationships. Has several individuals who can be relied upon for help. Is loved.	Many personal and professional relationships. Is loved.	Large number of personal and professional relationships. Has been mentored and has mentored others.

(continued on next page)

Employee Resource Continuum (continued)

	0	1
Hidden Rules of Class at Work	Knows and uses hidden rules of street at work.	Knows and uses hidden rules of hourly wages at work.
Desire and Persistence	Low energy. Not motivated. Does not want to be promoted. Dislikes learning. Quits often.	Selective energy but maybe not at work. Works for the money. Does not seek promotion. Avoids training. Gives up easily.

Adapted from Krabill/Payne Resource Quotient

The employee resource continuum analyzes the strengths of employees and identifies areas where mentoring between supervisors and employees might be useful. Building up resources in this way opens opportunities to create stability for the individual and the employer. The resource continuum also works hand in hand with the hidden talent quadrant model to help identify seemingly unlikely candidates for promotion who may actually be ready.

Teresa – A Case Study

Imagine Teresa is one of your employees. Analyze her resources and instead of losing her as an employee, determine what supports can be provided at work or outside of work to help Teresa stabilize her life so she can grow as an employee. When an employer helps stabilize Teresa's environment, they are also stabilizing their business. Using the chart, assess Teresa's resources.

2	3	4
Knows and uses hidden rules that members of mid-management follow at work.	Knows and uses hidden rules that officials at executive level follow at work. Knows hidden rules of country club.	Knows and uses hidden rules that are followed in corporate boardroom and with charities. Understands organizational, social, and business pedigree and hierarchy.
Steady energy. Motivated by need to be personally right. Controls information. Wants to be promoted for the power. Attends training.	High energy. Motivated by need to be organizationally correct. Seeks out training. Promotion or rewards desired for recognition.	High energy. Motivated by challenge. Promotion or rewards reflect excellence. Constantly learning on their own. Very persistent.

Employee Resources Review: Teresa

Teresa was hired as an assembly line worker in a factory. English was her second language when she came to the United States 25 years ago. Attractive and always stylish and colorful in dress, she has great manual dexterity. Her reading and writing skills are somewhat limited, and she still has difficulty taking directions in written English. But if you show her how to do something, she can do it immediately.

Teresa, 48, was married three times—the first two to very difficult men whom she supported financially. In addition, she had several live-in boyfriends along the way. Her third marriage—to Chico—helped her gain ground and reach financial stability; i.e., she could live from paycheck to paycheck. Teresa and Chico divorced two years ago. She has three grown children, two from different fathers, and two of her grandchildren live with her. She has also taken in foster children from time to time. Teresa was raised in extreme poverty and views her life with a high degree of fatalism, yet she is active in her neighborhood church. In short, her belief system seems to be a mix of roll-the-dice fate and Christian faith.

When Teresa's children had difficulties, she was always there to support them, just as she readily helps anyone in need. Of Teresa, people say, "She has a heart of gold." Not surprisingly, she has a network of people she can count on.

Teresa's emotional responses to colleagues vary, but she maintains great loyalty to the person who hired her.

Integrity	
Financial	
Emotional	
Mental	
Spiritual	
Physical	
Support system	
Relationships	
Hidden rules	
Motivation and persistence	
Language/ formal register	
TOTAL	

You Are the Supervisor

Teresa came to you recently to tell you there was a problem with one of the products. When you asked her what was wrong, she said, "I can't say exactly, but I can feel it." That is all she could articulate for you. You have learned you must be careful with your comments to Teresa. She is very proud, and any negative comment is usually viewed as personal criticism. In fact, when specifics of a product were discussed a few months ago, she told you it was "close enough." When you explained that close enough was not good enough, she seemed offended.

Keeping in mind that you don't know the whole story, what can you tell about Teresa just from reading this case study?

Integrity: It appears she has integrity.

Financial: Teresa, living paycheck to paycheck, is in daily instability.

Emotional: It seems like Teresa has some emotional swings. Everyone has worked with those who are always emotionally steady, and it's nice to know what to expect. I think everyone has worked with the opposite as well! I worked with a director of maintenance and buildings years ago whose mood was always unpredictable. When someone approached him with a need, they first took the department head's emotional temperature for the day and *then* figured out if and how they would get their need met.

When I managed bookstores, I used to call the administrative assistant of a particular department head to check the department head's emotional state before I contacted him directly. If his emotional resources were not high that day, I would call him another time.

Mental/Cognitive: The case study mentions that although language issues sometimes arise, Teresa is a quick study when a task is demonstrated. It's important not to confuse language/formal register resources with mental/cognitive resources.

Spiritual: She believes in a higher being and is active in her church. She views life in terms of fate instead of choice.

Physical: Teresa appears to have physical health and mobility with no difficulties.

Social Capital/Support System: She has good children, has been a foster parent, and has a solid network of friends.

Relationships/Role Models: Teresa has a network of friends and a good relationship with her supervisor.

Knowledge of Hidden Rules: It is safe to assume Teresa has learned some hidden rules she didn't grow up with, but her "good enough" quality control indicates that there are still some hidden rules of the workplace that she isn't using.

Motivation and Persistence: It is difficult to be sure, but it appears that she is motivated and persistent in life and work.

Language/Formal Register: Teresa has trouble using formal register in English. Instead she uses casual register and a circular story structure—not the language of business.

One of the issues for people like Teresa in the workforce is the development of resources that include language, knowledge of hidden rules, and role models.

The big issue at hand in this case study is that when something is wrong with one of the products, Teresa can't articulate what it is. She knows something is wrong, but she doesn't have the words to explain the issue. The use of questions to sort through the issues, along with other physical, tangible, visible steps and processes, will help Teresa's supervisor figure out what is wrong with the product.

English classes, financial literacy classes, and an investigation into the hidden rules of class would all be training that would benefit Teresa and help stabilize business operations. Not only does training like this provide more stability to Teresa within and outside of your employment, it also helps stabilize your business.

As team members receive promotions and accept new roles, they need to understand the hidden rules of those roles and those new levels of the business, whether it is a mid-level management position or an executive

Demands of Workplace Positions[50]

Issue	Daily Instability Entry Level	←
Knowledge level	What I can do.	What I can get others to do.
Responsibilities	Completion of tasks.	Completion of group tasks. Recommendations about hiring and firing.
Connections	Connections/ camaraderie within group.	With your immediate boss and the group you are supervising.
Protocol/culture	Accepted norms of immediate working group.	Mix of what the boss wants and the norms of the group.
Financial	Only as it relates to specific tasks.	Only as it relates to group task.
Planning	Daily, if any.	Planning for group tasks and task delegation.
Time commitment	For hours paid.	Some overtime.
Schooling	High school diploma or less.	High school or some college.*
Relocation	Not required.	Not required.
Technical expertise	Not required but desirable.	Recommended.

*Increasingly, two years of college is becoming a requirement for many occupations.

position. The same goes with resources: The more demands the position makes, the more resources people must have to meet the demands and be successful in that position.

Carol, an executive at a media company, told me she recognized early in her career that to climb the ladder, she needed to understand the hidden rules of the boardroom and use them to build the resources required by the kinds of positions she wanted.

Long-Term Stability **Executive Level**	
What I know.	Who I know.
Completion of projects and implementation of processes. Authority to hire and fire.	Identification of systems, products, services, and processes within business unit and among other related business units.
Internal connections up, down, and across organization crucial to success.	External connections vital to success of business unit.
Corporate hierarchy observed and followed.	National and often international social and business protocols observed and followed.
Departmental budget.	Profit and loss of business unit. Global strategic sales/revenues.
Weekly to annual. Project management.	Strategic. Quarterly to multi-year.
50–60 hours a week.	Position involves spouse, social activities, and extensive travel 60–80 hours a week.
Often a couple of years of college or college degree.	Often MBA.
May be required.	Required.
Use of specific software applications required.	Understanding and use of technical systems as they relate to strategic and financial success of business unit.

(continued on next page)

Demands of Workplace Positions (continued)

Issue	Daily Instability Entry Level	→
Communication	Mostly spoken, some written.	Responds in writing to written reports.
Spouse or significant other	Does not matter.	Does not matter.
Appearance	Needs to be somewhat clean.	Clean and presentable.

The information in this chart gives an indication of the demands of a position. It is a progression. Each level of the progression requires a higher level of resources. This information is not only helpful to supervisors working to promote their employees, it can help you personally as you climb the ladder.

Sometimes employees need to be taught what they need to do to be successful within the workplace. A few ways to do this are with onboarding, on-the-job training, and mentoring programs for newly promoted individuals. One of the earliest adaptors of this work implemented a "buddy system" when they retooled their business practices based on what they learned about the environment of daily instability. They paired a seasoned coworker with each new employee, which helped create stability for the new employee. After implementing this intervention, the employer retained more new employees past the critical 90-day mark. When employees are supported, they will achieve for the business.

→	Long-Term Stability Executive Level
Produces written reports. Makes reports/presentations to peers, customers, subordinates, and executive level.	Analyzes corporate documents for effect/ purpose. Makes reports/presentations to stakeholders.
Helpful but not crucial to career success.	Often determines whether promotion is given or not. Seen to reflect on person's judgment. Is reflection of personal choice.
Wears good-quality clothing that follows company norms and expectations. Clothing is pressed, neat, and clean.	Look is understated. Quality of haircut or hairstyle extremely important.

When employees' resources are built up in many areas, they will be capable of more autonomy and self-supervision at work. Fred Keller at Cascade is very proud of one of their plants that operates as a self-managed work team. Keller says he likes to see them "working as a team and building trust through the plant and the people to manage the safety and equality and scheduling issues so that you don't need to have someone telling you what to do." The self-management model empowers the employees to fix problems happening in the plant and provides them opportunities to grow into new areas of knowledge and expertise. This stability-building strategy at Cascade is about replacing standard work with the next level of improvement and involving all the employee ranks to accomplish it. Chapter 7 will look at more strategies that businesses can implement today to start building employee resources and stabilizing environments to boost the bottom line.

Business
Perspective

"When we implement stability strategies, employees feel valued, so they tend to be more dedicated. It improves morale."

"At the end of the day it's just good business because happy employees equal happy clients."

Employee
Perspective

"Now that I've examined economic class, I am able to see people at work in different ways, and I have more courage to approach those who are of a different economic class than me."

"One of the biggest stability factors my employer does for me is communicating with me as a person and making me feel important as a team member. Hearing my voice, giving me positive encouragement for a job well done, and asking for my thoughts for how to make the job more efficient all make it worth it for me to stay in this job."

CHAPTER 7

Now What? Strategies for Improving Retention, Productivity, and Profits

So far I have have discussed the environment of daily instability and how time is spent when people live in the tyranny of the moment. Issues can arise regarding hidden rules and language, but determining the level of someone's resources in a given area can give employers an advantage. Now let's discuss how to support employees, increase productivity, and create engagement, which ultimately drives stability and profitability for the company.

Exploring Company Culture, Best Practices, and Operational Excellence

Organizational and operational excellence and investing in employees will lead to increased value to customers, increased labor productivity, growth, profits, continuous improvement, return on investment, and more. It is the goal of this section to look at strategies for improving retention, productivity, and profitability by looking at best practices in specific ways that can stabilize employees through internal processes and programs.

Josh Bersin, the principal and founder of Bersin by Deloitte, has shared nine predictions on the future of human resources in the workplace. Two of the top three are directly applicable to the discussion of entry-level, lower-wage workers living in daily instability. Bersin's first prediction is that "culture, diversity, engagement, and retention will be front-burner issues."[51] While the article is looking at this through the traditional diversity of lenses—race, gender, culture, and engagement—perceptive businesses leaders will see how this prediction also holds true for entry-level, lower-wage employees coming from daily instability.

Bersin's third prediction is already taking place: "More companies will deal with overwhelmed employees."[52] By "overwhelmed" Bersin means that employees are overworked, overstimulated by devices, and have too much to do in too short a timeframe. This can also be applied to individuals living in daily instability: They are overwhelmed, living in the tyranny of the moment, solving problems only for today. Bersin recommends considering workplace flexibility, simplifying processes, and bringing more balance to the daily grind of work and life.[53] These approaches are also effective with entry-level, low-wage employees who are living in a concrete world and solving problems for today only.

In the book *The Good Jobs Strategy,* Zeynep Ton talks about how the smartest companies invest in their employees to reduce costs and boost net income. How? They do this by continually reviewing the processes and structures within all aspects of the business to make sure they are driving operational effectiveness and efficiency. Ton recommends concentrating on four areas:

Offer less – Instead of being all things to all customers all the time, offering less might mean operating with fewer hours, minimal or no sales/promotions, or fewer products. The key is to focus on how offering less can mean more for the employee base.

Standardize and empower – Don't take decisions away from employees; rather, combine standardization with empowerment, which allows for high efficiency and is adaptive to customers' needs.

Cross-train – Change what employees do based on customer demand, as opposed to changing the number of employees, which creates unpredictable and erratic work schedules.

Operate with slack – Do not cut costs by understaffing; rather, overstaff, which creates improved customer service and reduces costs by allowing employees to be involved in continuous improvement.[54]

Yes, the budget is tight. Managers and HR personnel are told to do more with less. Done correctly and with the proper management approach, improved best practices that "develop and promulgate standards, coordinate decision-making, optimize service delivery, and … manage the workforce"[55] are possible while staying in the required budget.

Jim Connolly, a retired hospital CEO and president, told me, "We can make those that come into our entry-level positions much better employees by reducing some of the crisis in life at work. When they show up at work, they are much more focused to get things done. Employees become more stable, better rounded, and more engaged. Frankly, long-term, you get someone like that in the door and you can have an employee for 20 years who advances through the system and becomes a real leader. And in the process, if you have success, you now have a mentor for the next new employee."

This retired CEO's, Ton's, and Bersin's insights and strategies are on-target ways to redefine the workplace by strengthening employees and the company. The Workplace Stability strategy matrix on the next page is designed to address how each of the following areas impacts operational excellence.

The strategy matrix provides a new lens through which employers can look at recurring employee issues that are creating chaos in the workplace. In the top left corner of the matrix, write a recurring employee problem statement. Underneath that statement, determine what the objective is by solving the problem and choosing whether to start making changes today or in the future. Along the top of the strategy matrix, you can analyze whether the problem is determined by the environment, the hidden rules of class, the resources of employees, the business, the community, and more. This strategy matrix allows you to look at everything this book has talked about so far and put it all on one page for easy review.

Workplace Stability Strategy Matrix

Problem Statement: Employees engage in destabilizing problem solving (e.g. payday loans, paycheck advances), miss or quit work because they cannot pay for life-stabilizing expenses.	Builds Resources	Finds Hidden Talent	Reveals Hidden Rules	Teaches Language	What Can One Person Do? (Impact of Individuals on Each Other)	Other Company Goal
Objective: Develop and implement an employee loan program.						
Type: Benefit program	X	X				
Now, Next, Later? Now						
Projected Start Date — MM/DD/YYYY						

Benefit Programs Health insurance, retirement savings, tuition reimbursement, etc. Includes changes in benefits themselves and in how they are communicated.	**Training Programs** Training to HR; supervisors, managers, and other leaders; work teams. Updating training to reflect ideas and culture development. Interactions learned here, such as training front-line staff in "the rules" and formal register.
Policy Changes Flextime, attendance, discipline, etc. Policies that can be updated to respond effectively to diverse employee situations.	**Individual Interactions** Strategies for training or other ways to encourage new, relationship-building interactions.
Management Practices Employee orientation, performance appraisal/ management systems, management's execution of policies.	**Other**

Employers can also use this process to review the employee life cycle within the company and determine if benefit and training programs, policy changes, management practices, employee interactions, or other initiatives would help create stability for the employees, thus creating stability for the business. Often in the process of reviewing an individual employee's recurring issue, employers are able to identify a way to support stability for all employees.

The beauty of this at-a-glance matrix is that it shows in a quick scan which areas of the company should change to get the needed results.

Let's work through the bottom section of the matrix.

Benefits Programs

One of the ways employers can stabilize the employee base and the company is with benefits packages. These include health insurance, retirement savings, tuition reimbursement, short-term and long-term disability insurance, paid vacation, paid holidays, etc.

When employers review their benefits programs with the driving forces for employees in daily instability in mind, they may uncover different needs than they assumed. What benefits do companies need to *start* offering? The benefits packages that suit the achievement-oriented, abstract thinker living in daily stability might not include the benefits needed—or even wanted—by an employee living in daily instability.

Consider a 401(k) plan: It is pointless without a connection to a long-range future story, the kind that prevails in daily stability. People in daily instability often don't participate in that program because they are not planning for the future. This is not to say that employers should not contribute to a 401(k). Employers just need to recognize that entry-level employees may choose not to contribute.

I asked Jesse, an inventory specialist, which benefits helped stabilize him at work. He said, "For obvious reasons, affordable healthcare for myself and my family has been an important benefit of my job. I mean, let's face it, if you don't have health, then you really don't have anything." Jesse went on to say that he has been in many positions where he didn't have paid leave either, and employers often put immense pressure on him and other employees to remain at work when they had a sick child. Providing support and stability to the team member during this time reaps huge rewards for the employer moving forward.

Some nontraditional benefits I have seen work well:

- An employee loan/income advance program – Businesses that have done this have worked with a credit union to establish a fixed available loan amount for an employee. The payback amount is deducted from the paycheck. This keeps the employee at work and helps to stabilize life issues.

- On-site health clinic – Employees are in and out of the clinic in 20 minutes, and business productivity remains high. Because time spent at agencies, including health clinics, is a concern in daily instability, employees appreciate the convenience of receiving health checkups without having to travel across town.

- Partnering with a daycare to provide childcare for the second and third shifts – One company also negotiated rates with a daycare chain that operated throughout the city so that if employees' primary childcare fell through, they could drop their kids off at one of the partnering daycares at a predetermined, reduced rate.

- Transportation vouchers and/or subsidized bus passes.

- Subsidized lunches from the corporate cafeteria.

- A corporate garden – Can be included in the corporate wellness plan, with employees given time to unwind during breaks by pulling weeds, watering, and harvesting vegetables. The produce is used for department lunches and the leftovers divided up to be taken home by employees.

- Free tax preparation.

- Resource networks for employers – When multiple businesses, nonprofits, and local government agencies band together to provide resources for employees living in daily instability, the results are dramatic.

- An employee pool that shares sick or vacation days with other employees who have fallen on hard times.

Resource Networks for Employers

Many businesses have found that forming or joining resource networks for employers is a great way to build stability while lowering costs. A resource network is a shared resource of multiple businesses that provides job retention services, reduces demands on human resources departments, and offers work supports that are available to all employees but that target entry-level employees who are living in daily instability. When an employee maintains employment, everyone benefits, and that's the main aim of the resource network for employers: keeping employees on the job and productive.

To clarify, I talk generically about resource networks for employers that are regional in focus and support local businesses within a smaller geographic region or state. Each of these networks provides employer supports, and the components and offerings may be unique to that network. I also provide examples from Employer Resource Networks (ERNs) affiliated with the national organization ERN-USA. This nationwide network of ERNs in the United States provides standardized supports to all of its members.

Rhino Foods in Burlington, Vermont, is a producer of high-quality ice cream and other frozen desserts. Rhino is also a member of Working Bridges, a regional resource network for employers in the Burlington area that works to help stabilize employees' environments.

Working Bridges assists employees with financial literacy education, provides income-advance loans for employees with unexpected financial emergencies, and employs resource coordinators who help employees solve life issues that interfere with work. A resource coordinator may help arrange childcare, continuing education, eldercare, housing, and legal assistance—all so that the employee can achieve stability without being absent from work to spend time at social service agencies.[56] In fact, a member of ERN-USA in the Schenectady area in New York provides 34 different categories of support!

In a promotional video created by Rhino and Working Bridges that illustrates how the businesses in the resource network are being stabilized, the audience meets Tammy, a batter-maker at Rhino. When Tammy's water heater broke and flooded her mobile home, she faced some dilemmas. She knew she must replace the water heater quickly, but she didn't have the money, and she didn't know how she would deal with this issue before she had to go back to work. Luckily one of her coworkers told her about the income advance program that Rhino offered through the Working Bridges program. Tammy couldn't believe a credit union would advance her money with her credit score, but they did. Within 24 hours Tammy had the $750 she needed to purchase a new hot water heater and have it installed.[57]

Rhino is not alone in stabilizing employees. Best Cleaners, a member of the Schenectady Area Employer Resource Network, bought out their largest competitor and found that the employees who came with it, when compared with the original Best Cleaners employees, were a very different group with very different needs and issues. There was a lot of mistrust from the employee base. In the first year the employee turnover rate amongst the new employees was seven times the turnover rate of employees at the original location. Participating in the resource network for employers helped Best Cleaners turn the corner. The extra level of support and benefits employees can access through the network provides a new trust and makes employees happy. And as the business owner said at the start of the chapter, happy employees equal happy clients.

Most human resources personnel are not trained to be social workers. That is where the resource network can be a real benefit. The resource network enables employees to stabilize their problems while staying at work. The production line keeps moving, and less company time is used to deal with the issues because they are handled by a resource coach employed by the resource network.

Stabilizing the employees in each of these examples also stabilized the businesses. Employees are now more financially stable and have a better work-life balance. While they are at work, they are able to give more of themselves and be more productive.

Sunset Retirement Community in Michigan is a member of the Lakeshore Employers Resource Network (LERN), an ERN-USA affiliate. Sunset CEO Chad Tuttle is pleased with the way LERN helps the retirement center with employee retention by building up the skills of employees and fostering their ability to stick it out in a job that's now easier to like. In fact, according to ERN-USA's James Vander Hulst, 20% of the employees on average across its affiliates use the program in some way. Tuttle adds that "there is no cheaper investment for a greater return. The resource network allows you to put the dollars where they are needed most. The network doesn't pick winners or losers in the employee base; it can assist anyone. The resource assistance goes directly to the heart of what is needed with employees." Tuttle's staff are now more dedicated to the job, and that raises the quality of service he can provide to his client base.

Fully 70% of the Working Bridges income-advance loan recipients continue with a savings account after the loan is repaid and maintain an average balance of $384. Like Working Bridges, LERN also has an open loan program with a local credit union. Karin, a Sunset Retirement Community employee, needed reliable transportation quickly because her car died. Through the open loan program, she filled out paperwork and received $1,000 toward the purchase of another car. Employees who borrow through the program have their loan repayments deducted automatically from their paychecks. They are also encouraged to deduct a little extra that goes into a savings account each time the loan payment is deducted. In addition to repaying her loan on time every week, Karin is accumulating savings, which will help stabilize her in the next emergency and also builds up her credit rating. When the loan is repaid, Karin can continue to make the weekly deposits into her savings account.

The resource network programs also change the way employees look at their employers and how they talk about their employers in the community. There are many positive payoffs when employers find ways to stabilize their employees.

I spoke with a director from the healthcare industry whose organization is a member of a resource network for employers. In her words, the resource network allows employees experiencing instability to remain at work while solving problems. Before they joined the resource network, housing problems, addiction, and food insecurity caused many to leave work abruptly or take days off without notice. Were these employees just playing hooky from work? No. They were going from agency to agency for referrals to still more agencies that might help them meet basic needs. The resource network mitigates that. Not only does a resource specialist help employees meet needs, it provides a comfort to the employee to speak to someone during the natural workflow of the day. The resource network meets the person where they are physically located. Instability impacts the bottom line, and the resource network helps put a stop to that.

Jane Canale works for a member of the Schenectady Area Employer Resource Network, an ERN-USA affiliate that recognizes a 97% retention rate after one year for employees who have been coached. Jane said that they were not ready for the surpise bonus that came along with membership in the network: the partnerships that developed between the businesses in the network. Each business is different, but they share the common bond of similar employee issues. Jane gave me three examples of how each business has been strengthened:

Example 1 – Several of the employers applied for a grant with the local workforce development office at the community college. As a result, the employers paid just $25 per employee to get 100 employees trained in a two-day entry-level supervisor training.

Example 2 – The local city mission reached out at the holidays and offered employees in the resource network free Christmas presents if they were having difficult times. One staff member with three children told her success coach that it had been a really tough year. She hadn't gotten out the decorations that holiday season, but after receiving support through the resource network, she planned on getting the tree out that night when she went home.

Example 3 – Unemployment was low, so the businesses in the resource network pooled their resources to host a job fair. They reduced their marketing and advertising costs by sharing the costs amongst themselves.

Read more about how to implement a resource network by checking out ERN-USA.com. They have been helping stabilize businesses, communities, and individuals with innovative resource network solutions since 2008.

While resource networks provide the support employees need, which allows coworkers, supervisors, and human resources staff to meet the needs of the business, participants in the network also collaborate with each other and forge stronger alliances.

According to Jane, the ERN provides the businesses that participate with a feeling of success about the supports they can offer and the speed and efficiency with which they are able to assist employees—and each other.

Presentation Format

Review your company's benefits package presentation format, keeping in mind that employees from daily instability need more concrete language and visual tools. There are times when employees do not take advantage of the benefits package simply because of the way the information about it is delivered. Do the written descriptions of employee benefits work for those who rely on casual register and nonverbal communication? It is helpful to include graphics, step sheets, and to use video clips whenever possible. When creating these documents, think in terms of concrete, immediate steps and results, not abstract, long-range plans.

Review the benefits plan and discover: What is utilized by employees, and what is under-used? How might the business get more employees to take advantage of a 401(k) plan? Try illustrating the matching funds more concretely by including real dollar bills in enrollment sessions. Use statements like: "If you put in this dollar, the company puts one in too. After a certain period of time, they're both yours to keep."

Benefits Programs

What does my company offer? What should we offer?

✓ 1. Paid holidays

✓ 2. Paid sick days

3. 401(k) contributions

4. _____

5. _____

Policy Changes

Every business has an employee handbook that lays out the policies and procedures of the organization. If used properly, the handbook is an *abstract* blueprint for the human resources activities of the business. The question is: Which policies and procedures can/should be adapted and changed to accommodate the needs of employees from daily instability—without compromising the needs of the business?

Start by checking the education and training policies. Make sure employees have access to the supports they need so they can provide the results the company needs. Is the attendance policy meeting the business needs? If not, adapt your policies to expand flexibility for workers. Employees who are happy and stress free outside of work make happier and more productive employees while on the time clock.

> **Policy Changes**
>
> *What does my company offer? What should we offer?*
>
> ✓ 1. Workplace flexibility
>
> 2. Attendance policy
>
> ✓ 3. Education policy
>
> 4. _____
>
> 5. _____

Workplace Flexibility

According to researcher Betsy Gwin, workplace flexibility "is commonly defined as workers and their employers working together to decide how, when, and where work will be performed."[58] Gwin goes on to say that "flexibility is about an employee and employer making changes to when, where, and how a person will work to better meet individual and business needs."[59] The Workforce Flexibility 2010 initiative says flexibility should include "flexible work arrangements, time off, and career maintenance and reentry."[60]

Workplace flexibility is not about an employer randomly cutting hours, creating last-minute changes to shifts, assigning employees a different shift for each day of the week, or reducing hours to keep from having to provide benefits (or based on the slack time allotted to a task).

Jodie Levin-Epstein's research into flexible working schedules states that "in a two-year study of 1,400 workers, 70% of managers and 87% of employees reported that workplace flexibility enhanced productivity."[61] When businesses retain employees, shareholder returns can also increase. Other studies indicate that flexible work arrangements enhance retention. It stands to reason that when employers can help them better balance their work and personal lives, they will have happier, higher-contributing employees.

A colleague told me about an electronics manufacturer who had very rigid expectations about being on time to work. The employer had all kinds of explanations for these expectations. Managers would say to employees, "We're assembling the brains of computers, and we need to be precise about everything. If people aren't punctual, workstations will sit empty and teams won't operate well together," etc. Employees who were one minute late could lose their jobs.

Well, the company ran into trouble and couldn't give raises one year. In order to retain their employees, they decided to relax the schedule and offer flextime. Suddenly, instead of losing their jobs for being one minute late, employees could arrive at work anytime within a two-hour window and be considered on time. They could arrive early and take a two-hour lunch break if they wanted or needed to. Productivity and employee morale soared through the roof. The electronics manufacturer got a much better result than a mere cost of living raise would have garnered.

When I asked Renee, Getting Ahead graduate and restaurant worker, what the best thing her employer gave her was, she said flexibility of hours. I asked her what would happen if her employer was not flexible, and she said she had been in that situation with a prior employer. When she was on that job despite having a crisis to deal with, the situation would take her out of the workplace and into her own head. Renee is a single parent whose child has some behavioral issues, and the flexibility at work enables her to attend to the needs of her son. This, in turn, allows her to stay productive and focused when she is at work.

Employees in daily instability are dealing with immediate needs and making ends meet for today. If employees living in daily instability have some flexibility in their work schedules, it will reduce absenteeism, enhance productivity, and improve the customer experience. And don't forget higher profits! "Employee use of flexibility was found to result in significant savings due to reductions in overtime costs resulting from unscheduled absences."[62]

The workplace flexibility movement argues that the underlying principle in workplace flexibility is "control and choice ... giving workers more choice and control over their time in order to better accommodate their complex needs ... choice in location, control over the number of hours regularly worked, choice about schedules, and control over priorities in the work-life balance."[63]

This same movement would recommend flexibility in the areas of compressed work weeks, part-time schedules, use of self-scheduling systems, and telecommuting. Of course, each of these examples needs to be discussed and possibly tested to make sure it works for both the employer and the employee. It is all about workplace effectiveness that benefits employers and employees alike. If the benefits aren't mutual, the plan will not be successful.

Certainly there will be challenges to implementing workplace flexibility. First human resources will need to find a balance between the requests of the employees and the needs of the business. Secondly, the business must use the time of employees and managers effectively in developing work schedules and meeting the strategic needs of the company; there will be a fine line between the short request time and company coverage, especially because it is often the "tyranny of the moment" for employees from daily instability. Human resources will need to be involved to make sure employers are following HR guidelines between employees as they approve and deny requests. Lastly, achieving a quality customer experience that always provides customers with the level of service they've come to expect from the company is of key importance.[64]

Zeynep Ton's model for operational excellence, which includes operating with slack, cross-training employees, standardizing processes and procedures that empower employees, and offering less, goes a long way toward having a productive and engaged workforce. All of these approaches will provide the business operation with needed stability while allowing employees to deal with work-life issues.

Using the new lens to understand the driving forces for employees in daily instability, and with the strategy matrix in mind, what policy changes will benefit your business?

Management Practices

The corporate culture created by upper management affects day-to-day operation, employee motivation, and the processes, rhythms, and practices of employees and departments. The corporate culture includes promoting from within, placing value on employees as integral parts of the company, how work teams are set up and function, and even how performance appraisals are handled. Is upper management inclusive? What practices can be changed that will develop employees? How can shifts in management practices better serve the company and employees?

The more inclusive management is with the balance of power, the more productivity it will get from employees. Look for common ground with employees, whether that is language, common skills, experiences, status, or mental attributes. Examine the style or level of communication between executives, supervisors, and entry-level employees, and make sure to use words that can be understood by all employees. In other words, make sure all employees can understand the written and spoken language used in the business. A company can't use only abstract thoughts and ideas when there are concrete thinkers in the ranks.

> **Management Practice Changes**
>
> *What does my company offer? What should we offer?*
>
> ✓ 1. Revised/new employment orientation
>
> 2. Adapted performance reviews
>
> 3. _____

When I asked Jesse, a Getting Ahead graduate, what he would like the company to do that they weren't doing already, he said, "I would like an 'employee think tank' where all the leaders of crews and departments would sit down without the managers to discuss what would help the company and the employees. We would roll it into a list and then sit down with management to discuss. I want people in management to listen to employees' opinions." And why wouldn't employers do this? Employees who work the process day in and day out can see where inefficiencies are occurring, and businesses should harness that strength.

New-employee orientation can be an off-putting experience to someone from daily instability. In the ideal, what do businesses want to achieve with orientation? Of course they want the traditional transfer of knowledge about job expectations, but what about relationship building? What does your organization need to do to accomplish that in its new-employee orientation process?

One employer realized there was way too much abstract information passed along during the first week of employment. Many new hires didn't come back for the second week, and it was expensive and wasteful investing so much time in employees who didn't stay. When the company realized that the people from daily instability who applied for the job were being overwhelmed by the multitude of abstract information, they revamped their orientation to address more concrete aspects of what the job actually requires on a daily basis. The company split the orientation into three parts, giving employees what they needed to get started and separating out some things that could be taught later. They also changed how they delivered the training; they focused on how to teach concretely some of their policies and procedures and gave examples through stories, videos, and infographics.

For best results in orientation and onboarding, consider directly teaching employees phrases that are needed to do the job, be mindful of the different language experiences and needs of the employees, describe in concrete terms what needs to be done, and focus on concrete steps using videos, pictures, step sheets, and other tools.

What does the company currently offer, and what does it need to change to achieve more internal stability?

Training Programs

As I've noted, "the value of hourly and lower-wage employees to many organizations is only expected to increase in the future. Demographic changes in the United States workforce mean that traditional sources of qualified personnel are less likely to provide an adequate number of skilled entry-level workers … *In order to stay competitive in an increasingly global economy, employers will need to hire, train, and retain entry-level personnel.*"[65]

I'm sure this isn't a reality readers are eager to hear about, much less eager to embrace. But in order to be an industry leader, it is necessary to expand the training provided to new hires and to employees throughout their employment.

Getting Ahead in the Workplace

I recommend that businesses also train their employees living in daily instability on the hidden rules of class, resources, and language. There are many ways to do this, and aha! Process can work directly with an organization to analyze its practices and provide guidance. Two of the models that have been very successful are Getting Ahead in a Just-Gettin'-By World[66] and its offshoot, Getting Ahead in the Workplace.[67] (both referred to as "Getting Ahead" for short.) The Getting Ahead model, created by author Philip DeVol, takes the information about the environments of individuals—the mental models of instability and stability, the hidden rules of class, the resources, and the registers of language—and puts it into a concrete delivery format. The purpose of Getting Ahead is to help employees investigate their economic reality for themselves so they can make their own decisions about what they will do to build stability in their lives.

"My company can't afford to offer this kind of training during working hours," you might be thinking. DeVol actually recommends partnering with a local nonprofit to offer the training off site. This takes the professional development out of the workplace environment, away from human relations employees or supervisors who might want to monitor the interactions, comments, or processes of the employees in Getting Ahead. Another way to offer Getting Ahead is through the resource network for employers. This could mean employees would get the chance to participate in Getting Ahead with employees from other firms in the network.

Offering Getting Ahead as an employee training option provides a way for employees to plan for and create stability in their lives. Employees deserve the opportunity to explore economic class and gain access to the same information driving changes in the workplace now that the employer's paradigm has shifted.

The following are comments I heard from employees who have completed the Getting Ahead process of investigating instability:

> *"Since completing Getting Ahead, I don't feel threatened, and I'm more confident in conversations. If I disagree with a manager, I can communicate that disagreement and not be abrasive."*

> *"Now that I understand the 'why' of middle class, it took my hate away."*

> *"I have the ability to look at life through a new, nonjudgmental lens. I have a framework to use for how I want my life to become."*

> *"Before Getting Ahead, I didn't have the tools I needed to reach out to a supervisor and get the help I needed. I would walk away from a job. Getting Ahead has given me the ability to reach out and communicate better with my manager. I handle things better now."*

> *"Before, I didn't see my life going anywhere. Now I don't see a ceiling. My world is so good, and my kids have greater opportunities."*

A recent study conducted by Elizabeth Wahler of the Indiana University School of Social Work finds that the Getting Ahead model appears to be effective with individuals who have "multiple and complex barriers to economic mobility and stability."[68] The report goes on to say that Getting Ahead facilitates positive changes with individuals living in daily instability as it relates to "perceived stress, mental health and well-being, social support, self-efficacy, hope, and goal-directed behavior and planning."[69] As an employer, what isn't to like about all of these stabilizing factors for those employees living in the tyranny of the moment, reacting to problems of the day, not planning for tomorrow, and creating chaos within workflow and processes?

Workplace Stability Employee Training

The interview in Chapter 4 with Fred Keller, CEO of Cascade Engineering, details how he recognized that he needed to extend economic diversity training to all of his employees. Race and gender compliance are at the forefront of the business conversation, but rarely if ever do businesses discuss how the environment of economic class affects workflow, productivity, and dollars. To recognize the successes businesses are looking for, the entire team should be trained on economic diversity in the workplace.

Training Ideas That Have Worked for Others

These recommendations may not be what employers traditionally think about when they plan their internal training programs, but these strategies have proven effective for businesses that lead their fields in competitive advantage and employee retention.

- Tuition reimbursement – Because tuition reimbursement is traditionally thought of as money for graduate degrees, businesses miss opportunities to include a GED class, financial literacy class, or technical skills class offering that would support systems. I recommend collaboration with local community colleges and technical schools to offer courses that meet the direct needs of your specific business and employee base.

- One employer provides all employees with an annual allowance of $1,500 to spend on learning. Books, courses, and certifications all count. The intent is that employees will strengthen their skills for the job and may even prepare for advancement. Another employer offers $5,200 per year for work-related education. Regardless of the amount, a business should do what it can based on available budgets and the practices of the competition.

- A healthcare employer with a continuing education tuition reimbursement program found that the policies didn't allow them to reimburse an employee for the cost of a GED course. They realized immediately that this was bad policy, and they acted quickly to change it—after reimbursing the employee who made the initial request.

- Another employer uses a monthly book club approach to address topics such as bullying in the workplace. Using this facilitated approach, the employer is covering sensitive but important topics.

- Basic computer literacy classes have proven effective for employees whose main exposure to technology is via their mobile phones.

- Home ownership classes with an emphasis on caring for a home can help people create future stories where they have made the transition to daily stability or even long-term stability.

No matter what kinds of training programs a business offers, it can support employee skill development in these two ways: (1) embed the needed job tasks and strategies into daily instructions and briefing content, and (2) directly teach job tasks that have not been mastered.

Instead of assuming that employees come into employment ready to make use of data and information, employers must start by supplying the information to employees in ways that demonstrate how the business wants them to use it. Embed these strategies right away, starting with onboarding. The same approach then needs to be followed when teaching someone a new role/position in the company.

Training Programs

What does my company offer?
What should we offer?

✓ 1. Tuition reimbursement for any course

2. Getting Ahead in the Workplace

3. Training for employees on economic class

4. _____

5. _____

If employees are not ready to make use of a business's data and information—to adapt to that company's ways of doing business—then employers need to teach them directly, perhaps showing them how to complete a task. Demonstrate the concrete pieces so employees can see the work being done, and at the same time weave the abstract concepts in along the way. A process like this helps employees develop a sense of pride in their work while creating the productivity businesses are looking for.

Individual Interactions

When I asked Renee what she wanted from her employer that she wasn't getting, she said, "I want my employer to communicate with me more." She wanted her manager, supervisor, and the business as an entity to understand her and make her feel more involved. In her words, "If you involve employees and make them feel valued, they will give their best to you."

A goal should be to improve relationships between employees and management. Many strategies that improve and strengthen relationships take no money and little effort. Employees living in the daily reality of the tyranny of the moment value relationships very highly and will definitely work harder for someone they respect. Whether it is a benefit program, a policy change, a management practice, a training program—anything—businesses will get greater buy-in, motivation, and productivity when they develop relationships of mutual respect with their employees.

In order to reinforce the idea that employees are respected, one employer instituted a "call before you quit" policy. Employees sign an agreement stating they will call a designated number before walking off the job and deciding not to come back. The number rings someone in human relations who helps the employee find a solution to the problem that is making them want to quit. Many times reaching out to someone and talking through the issue at hand, whether it is emotional, financial, etc., helps the employee recognize that quitting will not help. Several employers have replicated this approach, and they all achieve very high rates of retention.

A resource network for employers usually features at least one shared employee called a resource manager/coordinator or success coach who helps employees work through issues. Many times employees who are building stability and working to balance work-life issues develop a deep level of trust with the resource manager. These relationships then become tools for developing more meaningful interactions with individual employees.

Individual Interactions

What does my company offer? What should we offer?

✓ 1. A plan to improve communication

2. Relationship-building interaction

3. _____

Joyce Gutierrez-Marsh, the Department of Human Services case manager who provides support to Michigan resource network The SOURCE, says the best part of her role is working directly with employees. In her role she builds trust and relationships that enable her to help employees remove barriers better and faster than anyone else in the organization. Managers and supervisors who build this kind of rapport with employees will achieve increased retention and productivity with their teams.

A supervisor in Texas worked with employees from daily instability to help them understand how to read their bank statements. People in daily stability consider direct deposit to be a great benefit. They don't have to take the check to the bank; they can be out of the country or on vacation, and their funds are still deposited. However, a person who grew up in a family that was unbanked, living without the use of checking and savings accounts, probably won't know how to read a bank statement without a mentor. The supervisor in Texas not only saw the stability benefits of working with his team on basic financial literacy that business leaders often take for granted, he was also able to build relationships of mutual respect along the way.

Yet another reason for working to improve individual interactions is to enhance employee performance appraisals. Having strong relationships built on mutual respect and trust allows for healthy exchanges during performance appraisals (and during disciplinary actions, should they become necessary). Amber Werner, a program director, told me that her first employee evaluation ended in tears. She felt like her boss didn't like her and gave her what she perceived to be criticism. She now recognizes that it was constructive feedback meant to mentor her in growing her resources, but based on that experience, her boss changed the way evaluations are handled with entry-level employees. Relationships are the driving force. Build on them!

What changes and enhancements to individual interactions can be made in your business?

The components of the Workplace Stability strategy matrix evaluate the employee life cycle through the eyes of low-wage employees. Leaders who look at business through this economic lens can use the insights to define and create changes as needed to stop recurring problems that plague the workplace with absenteeism, low productivity, conflict, workflow processes breaking down, etc. Then they will have started on their way to stabilizing the business to get the results they are looking for, results that will improve the business without lowering standards, expectations, or net income.

Get started now. What recurring problem is your company experiencing?

Workplace Stability Strategy Matrix

Problem Statement: Employees engage in destabilizing problem solving (e.g. payday loans, paycheck advances), miss or quit work because they cannot pay for life-stabilizing expenses.	Builds Resources	Finds Hidden Talent	Reveals Hidden Rules	Teaches Language	What Can One Person Do? (Impact of Individuals on Each Other)	Other Company Goal
Objective: Develop and implement an employee loan program.						
Type: Benefit program						
Now, Next, Later? Now						
Projected Start Date MM/DD/YYYY						

Benefit Programs	Training Programs
Policy Changes	Individual Interactions
Management Practices	Other

CHAPTER 8

Workplace Model

The components of this model create ideal conditions for the retention, engagement, and increased productivity of entry-level employees.

Workplace Stability is the book you are reading and its accompanying training, which explore the retention, productivity, and engagement of entry-level employees who live in an environment of daily instability. This information is key for executives and mid-level managers, and variations can be used with all employees. By changing the way they do business to embrace the diversity of their employees' environments, employers can generate stability, halt employee turnover, and enjoy the resulting increase in productivity—and net income. aha! Process offers training solutions on this content.

Getting Ahead in the Workplace is a program that helps entry-level employees living in instability investigate their economic realities. In the process of investigating, employees decide for themselves how they will begin to build their resources and take control of their future stories.

This 16-session program is best facilitated with a community partner so that employees are free to explore and investigate without a supervisor or human resource manager listening in. Daily instability is painful to examine, and in this process the employees need to know they are in a safe, neutral environment.

Many times employees who complete Getting Ahead will comment that they didn't know their lives could be different. Graduates of Getting Ahead have gotten rid of their debt, gone back to college, purchased their first homes—all because they gained tools to plan for the future. Many graduates say Getting Ahead helped them understand the hidden rules of stability. Understanding and using these rules, which guide the operations of achievement-based businesses, increases employees' social capital and makes them more receptive to the formal language business depends on every day.

Some businesses offer Getting Ahead as a training program for any employee, and some have added it to the wellness menu as an option. Learn more about how to implement and train on Getting Ahead in the Workplace online at ahaprocess.com.

Human Resources Redesign is an integral part of the model. After an employer's paradigm shifts to examining the environment of instability and its impact on the success of the business, they will need to create changes internally to get the results they are looking for. The employee life cycle needs to be examined, and internal changes to onboarding, management practices, benefits, training, evaluations, and more need to be considered. aha! Process is happy to walk beside business teams of all sizes as they modify their existing business practices to maximize stability, employee retention, and profits.

Hidden Rules of Class at Work is a book and workshop that looks at how class issues help determine one's ability to be successful in the workplace. Based on the Krabill/Payne Resource Quotient, an assessment tool for employers, the book's purpose is twofold: It is useful if you are looking for a promotion yourself, and it offers strategies for managing, mentoring, and promoting employees from diverse economic environments. The hidden rules of economic class and the hidden rules of the workplace often intersect in surprising ways, but the power of these rules can be harnessed and used for achievement by employers and employees alike. Learn more about Hidden Rules of Class at Work at ahaprocess.com.

Public-Private Partnership

Participating in a **resource network for employers** is a way to create partnerships with community nonprofits and provide new resources to employees that are outside a company's ability to provide as an employer alone. It is an effective way to keep employees working while providing them the means to solve the life issues that occur in the daily tyranny of the moment. James Vander Hulst and his team at **ERN-USA** provide guidance, consulting, and assistance to businesses searching for workforce stability through innovative practices. Members of Lakeshore ERN are recognizing retention rates of 99% of those who have been coached and have stayed in the job for 12 months, achieving a return on investment of 342%, and have supported 244 distinct employees and leveraged $52,534 in community resources.[70]

An organization might want to adopt the ERN-USA model, as ERN-USA has the broadest national network of employers in the United States. Alternatively, a business might find a regional network in its area that provides collaborative public-private workplace partnerships. Whomever a business partners with, one of the key elements of a network is a resource manager who rotates between participating businesses to help resolve the life obstacles that keep employees from being fully productive at work. The businesses in essence buy shares of this resource manager's time as part of their participation in the resource network, and the resource manager spends a set number of hours per week at each business to support employees. This arrangement reduces demands on managerial and human resources staff and allows them to concentrate on strategic matters. The relationship and trust created between the resource manager and employees are integral to the success of the network.

One of the fastest ways to stabilize employees is by offering **small dollar loans** in partnership with banks and credit unions. When employees have quick access to small dollar loans at affordable interest rates, they are better able to deal with emergencies that might otherwise keep them from work. A payroll deduction that repays the loan automatically makes it easier for employees to manage finances moving forward, and it often leads to a savings plan when the loan has been repaid.

Community Involvement

Bridges Out of Poverty is a book, a movement, a workshop, and a set of strategies to provide stability in communities. Workplace Stability is rooted in the core philosophies of Bridges and reframes its core constructs for business. Bridges uses a "triple lens" to look at the environment of poverty at the individual, organizational, and community levels. To truly stabilize a community, the issues identified using each lens must be addressed. As a business partners with community members and organizations to stabilize employees, Bridges is the component of the model the community will embrace. Find out more about about implementing and training on Bridges at ahaprocess.com.

The more components of the model are embedded with employees, supervisors, and community members, the more stability will be created in the business and the community. It is with this stability that a business can continue to be competitive in its marketplace. The goal is to create communities where all live well and where schools, community organizations, and businesses thrive today and tomorrow.

CONCLUSION

Viewing a diverse workforce through the lens of economic class allows a company to create more stability for team members and for the business, which results in higher retention, higher productivity, more engagement, and increased profits. Business is about fulfilling a passion and meeting a need, but in the end, business is also about profitability and the ability to meet short-term needs like payroll and achieve long-term goals. That requires long-term stability and profitability.

I hope that these insights into the hidden rules, resources, and language patterns of daily instability and daily stability have opened up ideas and strategies that will take your business to another level of success.

I challenge you not just to read this book and say, "Oh, interesting," but to take the time, the work, and the energy to create a more accepting workplace for employees who are struggling with instability. Be more inclusive of the employee base living in daily instability. Trust the success of those businesses that have gone before you. Your company will reap huge rewards, not only financially, but with improved retention, productivity, and other great results you never even expected.

ENDNOTES

Introduction
[1]Mullainathan & Shafir, 2013, p. 4
[2]Payne, 1995, 2013
[3]Bradley, 2003
[4]Payne, DeVol, & Dreussi-Smith, Bridges Out of Poverty, 1999
[5]Payne, DeVol, & Dreussi-Smith, Bridges Out of Poverty, 2009
[6]In some cases names and job details have been changed.
[7]DeVol, 2015a, 2015b

Chapter 1
[8]Bond & Galinksy, 2006
[9]Payne, 2013
[10]Litchfield, Swanberg, & Sigworth, 2004, p. 5
[11]The Economist Intelligence Unit, 2014, p. 7
[12]Ibid.
[13]Giuffrida, 2015
[14]Blake, 2006
[15]Derr & Holcomb, 2010
[16]"Employer Resource Network," 2016

Chapter 2
[17]Payne, 2013, p. 133
[18]Ibid., p. 43
[19]Gwin, 2011, p. 276
[20]Adapted from DeVol, 2010, pp. 13–16
[21]Shipler, 2004, p. 27
[22]Desmond, 2015
[23]National Coalition for the Homeless, 2007
[24]"America's Fortunes," 2004, n.p.
[25]Shipler, 2004, p. 40
[26]Sapolsky, 1998, p. 301; Sapolsky, 2005
[27]Lareau, 2003, p. 28
[28]Addy, Engelhardt, & Skinner, 2013
[29]"America's Fortunes," 2004, n.p.
[30]Putnam, 2000, p. 317
[31]Ibid., p. 319

[32]Lareau, 2003, p. 15
[33]Goodman, 2003, pp. 137–158
[34]"Food Desert Statistics," n.d.

Chapter 3
[35]Silverman, 2012
[36]Ibid.
[37]Society for Human Rights Management, 2014
[38]Payne, DeVol, & Dreussi-Smith, 2009

Chapter 5
[39]ProLiteracy, 2014
[40]ProLiteracy, 2003
[41]Hart & Risley, 1995
[42]ProLiteracy, 2003
[43]Ibid., p. 8
[44]Ibid.
[45]Maria Montano-Harmon, 1991
[46]Sibbet, 2013
[47]Ibid. p. 38
[48]Berne, 1996.
[49]Payne & Krabill, 2002
[50]Ibid.

Chapter 7
[51]Bersin, 2015a, n.p.
[52]Bersin, 2015b, n.p.
[53]Bersin, 2015c
[54]Ton, 2014
[55]Hoque, 2012
[56]Giuffrida, 2015
[57]Rhino Foods, 2011.
[58]Gwin, 2011, p. 266
[59]Ibid., p. 275
[60]Danziger & Boots, 2008, p. 1
[61]Levin-Epstein, 2006, p. 8
[62]Watson & Swanberg, 2011, p. 26
[63]Gwin, 2011, p. 266–267
[64]Danziger & Boots, 2008
[65]Litchfield, Swanberg, & Sigworth, 2004, p. 5, emphasis added
[66]DeVol, 2015a
[67]DeVol, 2015b
[68]Wahler, 2015, p. 6
[69]Ibid., p. 5

Chapter 8
[70]ERN-MI, 2016.

BIBLIOGRAPHY

Addy, S., Engelhardt, W., & Skinner, C. (2013). Basic facts about low-income children: Children under 18 years, 2011. National Center for Children in Poverty. Retrieved from http://nccp.org/publications/pdf/text_1074.pdf

America's fortunes [Editorial]. (2004). *The Atlantic, 293*(1). Retrieved from http://www.theatlantic.com/magazine/archive/2004/01/americas-fortunes/302859/

Becker, K., Krodel, K., & Tucker, B. (2009). *Understanding and engaging under-resourced college students.* Highlands, TX: aha! Process.

Berne, E. (1996). *Games people play.* New York, NY: Ballantine Books.

Bersin, J. (2015a, January 7). Prediction 1: Culture, diversity, engagement and retention will be front-burner issues. Retrieved from https://www.shrm.org/publications/hrmagazine/editorialcontent/2015/010215/pages/010215-hr-prediction-one.aspx

Bersin, J. (2015b, January 7). Prediction 3: More companies will deal with overwhelmed employees. Retrieved from https://www.shrm.org/publications/hrmagazine/editorialcontent/2015/010215/pages/010215-hr-prediction-three.aspx

Bersin, J. (2015c, January 7). What's in store for HR in 2015? Retrieved from http://www.shrm.org/publications/hrmagazine/editorialcontent/2015/010215/pages/010215-2015-predictions-for-hr.aspx

Bhargava, D. (2004, August 13). How much is enough? *The American Prospect, 15*(9). Retrieved from http://prospect.org/article/how-much-enough

Blake, R. (2006, July 17). Employee retention: What employee turnover really costs your company. Retrieved from http://ezinearticles. com/?Employee-Retention:-What-Employee-Turnover-Really-Costs-Your-Company-and-What-to-Do-About-It&id=245277

Bond, J. T., & Galinsky, E. (2006). How can employers increase the productivity and retention of entry-level, hourly employees? Families and Work Institute. Retrieved from http://familiesandwork.org/site/ research/reports/brief2.pdf

Bradley, J. R. (2003, spring). Bridging the cultures of business and poverty. *Stanford Social Innovation Review.* Retrieved from http://ssir. org/articles/entry/bridging_the_cultures_of_business_and_poverty

Danziger, A., & Boots, S. W. (2008). Lower-wage workers and flexible work arrangements. Workplace Flexibility 2010. Retrieved from http://workplaceflexibility2010.org/images/uploads/Lower-Wage%20 Workers%20and%20FWAs.pdf

Derr, M., & Holcomb, P. (2010, June). Issue brief: Employer resource networks. Social Policy Research Associates, Mathematica Policy Research. Retrieved from http://www.mathematica-mpr.com/~/media/ publications/PDFs/labor/WIRED_brief1.pdf

Desmond, M. (2015, March). Unaffordable America: Poverty, housing, and eviction. *Fast Focus.* Institute for Research on Poverty, University of Wisconsin – Madison. Retrieved from http://www.irp.wisc.edu/ publications/fastfocus/pdfs/FF22-2015.pdf

DeVol, P. E. (2010). *Bridges to sustainable communities: A systemwide, cradle-to-grave approach to ending poverty in America.* Highlands, TX: aha! Process.

DeVol, P. E. (2015a). *Getting ahead in a just-gettin'-by world: Building your resources for a better life* (3rd rev. ed.). Highlands, TX: aha! Process.

DeVol, P. E. (2015b). *Getting ahead in the workplace: Building stability and resources for a better life at work and home.* Highlands, TX: aha! Process.

Disruptive Innovations for Social Change. (n.d.). The DISC locator/ scaling tool for employer resource networks: Guidebook for dialogue and assessment. Retrieved from http://www.ern-usa.com/blob/site-files.ashx?ID=4

Dreier, P. (2000, summer). Why America's workers can't pay the rent. *Dissent,* 38–44. Retrieved from http://www.peterdreier.com/wp-content/uploads/2014/04/Why_Americas_Workers_Cant_Pay_the_ Rent.pdf

Duncan, G. J., & Brooks-Gunn, J. (Eds.). (1997). *Consequences of growing up poor.* New York, NY: Russell Sage Foundation.

The Economist Intelligence Unit. (2014, February). What's next: Future global trends affecting your organization: Evolution of work and the worker. SHRM Foundation. Retrieved from https://www.shrm.org/ about/foundation/shapingthefuture/documents/2-14%20theme%20 1%20paper-final%20for%20web.pdf

Employer resource network 2015 annual report breakfast. (2016, January 13). Retrieved from http://www.ern-ny.com/blob/news-files. ashx?ID=1004

ERN-MI. (2016). Lakeshore ERN (LERN). Retrieved from http://ern-mi. com/area-network.aspx?AreaID=1

Food desert statistics. (n.d.). Teaching Tolerance. Retrieved from http:// www.tolerance.org/sites/default/files/general/desert%20stats.pdf

Gallup. (2013). State of the global workplace. Retrieved from http:// www.gallup.com/services/178517/state-global-workplace.aspx

Giuffrida, I. (2015). The workplace as a platform for financial stability: A profile of Working Bridges, a project of United Way of Chittenden County. Retrieved from http://www.unitedwaycc.org/files/galleries/ Working_Bridges_Profile_FINAL.pdf

Goodman, L. (2003, December). A rotten deal. *Self.*

Gwin, B. (2011). Lessons for anti-poverty advocates from the workplace flexibility movement: Improving flexibility in low-wage work and access to work supports. *Georgetown Journal on Poverty Law and Policy, 18*(2), 265.

Hart, B. L., & Risley, T. R. (1995). *Meaningful differences in the everyday experience of young American children.* Baltimore, MD: Paul H. Brookes.

Hoque, F. (2012, November 7). The anatomy of operational excellence. Fast Company. Retrieved from http://www.fastcompany.com/3002767/anatomy-operational-excellence

Keegan, P. (2014/2015, December/January). The 5 new rules of employee engagement. Inc. Magazine. Retrieved from http://www.inc.com/magazine/201412/paul-keegan/the-new-rules-of-engagement.html

Kruse, K. E. (2012). *Employee engagement 2.0: How to motivate your team for high performance (a real-world guide for busy managers).* Seattle, WA: CreateSpace.

Lareau, A. (2003). *Unequal childhoods: Class, race, and family life.* Berkeley, CA: University of California Press.

Levin-Epstein, J. (2006, July). Getting punched: The job and family clock: It's time for flexible work for workers of all wages. Center for Law and Social Policy. Retrieved from http://www.clasp.org/resources-and-publications/files/0303.pdf

Litchfield, L. C., Swanberg, J. E., & Sigworth, C. M. (2004, April). Boston College Center for Work and Family Carroll School of Management. Retrieved from http://www.bc.edu/content/dam/files/centers/cwf/pdf/LowWageStudy.pdf

Mattera, P. (1990). *Prosperity lost.* Reading, MA: Addison-Wesley.

Montano-Harmon, M. R. (1991). Discourse features of written Mexican Spanish: Current research in contrastive rhetoric and its implications. *Hispania, 74*(2), 417–425.

Mullainathan, S., & Shafir, E. (2013). *Scarcity: Why having so little means so much.* New York, NY: Henry Holt.

National Coalition for the Homeless. (2007, June). Why are people homeless? NCH Fact Sheet #1. Retrieved from http://www.nationalhomeless.org/publications/facts/Why.pdf

Payne, R. K. (1995). *A framework for understanding poverty.* Baytown, TX: RFT.

Payne, R. K. (2013). *A framework for understanding poverty: A cognitive approach* (5th rev. ed.). Highlands, TX: aha! Process.

Payne, R. K., DeVol, P. E., & Dreussi-Smith, T. (1999). *Bridges out of poverty: Strategies for professionals and communities.* Highlands, TX: aha! Process.

Payne, R. K., DeVol, P. E., & Dreussi-Smith, T. (2009). *Bridges out of poverty: Strategies for professionals and communities* (4th rev. ed.). Highlands, TX: aha! Process.

Payne, R. K., & Krabill, D. (2002). *Hidden rules of class at work.* Highlands, TX: aha! Process.

ProLiteracy. (2003, March). U.S. adult literacy programs: Making a difference. Retrieved from http://literacyconnects.org/img/2011/11/US-Adult-Lit-Programs-Making-a-Difference-Research-review.pdf

ProLiteracy. (2014). The numbers don't lie. Retrieved from http://www.proliteracy.org/the-crisis/adult-literacy-facts

Public policy platform on flexible work arrangements. (n.d.). Workplace Flexibility 2010, Georgetown Law. Retrieved from http://workplaceflexibility2010.org/images/uploads/PublicPolicyPlatformonFlexibleWorkArrangements.pdf

Putnam, R. D. (2000). *Bowling alone: The collapse and revival of American community.* New York, NY: Simon & Schuster.

Rhino Foods. (2011). Working bridges [video]. Retrieved from https://vimeo.com/19870371

Sapolsky, R. M. (1998). *Why zebras don't get ulcers: An updated guide to stress, stress-related diseases, and coping.* New York, NY: W. H. Freeman.

Sapolsky, R. M. (2005, December 15). Sick of poverty. *Scientific American.* Retrieved from http://www.precaution.org/lib/06/prn_sick_of_poverty.051215.htm

Shipler, D. K. (2004). *The working poor: Invisible in America.* New York, NY: Alfred A. Knopf.

Sibbet, D. (2013). *Visual leaders.* Hoboken, NJ: Wiley.

Sigma Assessment Systems. (2016). Eguide: Improving employee retention in retail: Top 10 strategies. Retrieved from http://www. sigmaassessmentsystems.com/articles/empturnover.asp

Silverman, R. E. (2012, April 3). Is it better to promote from within? *Wall Street Journal.* Retrieved from http://www.wsj.com/articles/SB1 0001424052702304750404577320000041035504.

Society for Human Resource Management. (2014, May). Employee job satisfaction and engagement: The road to economic recovery. Retrieved from http://www.shrm.org/Research/SurveyFindings/ Documents/14-0028%20JobSatEngage_Report_FULL_FNL.pdf

Sweeney, D. (2013, February 11). 4 benefits of promoting within instead of hiring new employees. Retrieved from http://blog.mycorporation. com/2013/02/4-benefits-of-promoting-within-instead-of-hiring-new-employees/

Ton, Z. (2014). *The good jobs strategy: How the smartest companies invest in employees to lower costs and boost profits.* Seattle, WA: New Harvest.

Wahler, E. A. (2015, October 21). Getting ahead in a just-gettin'-by world: Program evaluation results. Retrieved from http://www. ahaprocess.com/wp-content/uploads/2015/10/GA-Program-Evaluation-Results.pdf

Watson, L., & Swanberg, J. E. (2011, May). Flexible workplace solutions for low-wage hourly workers: A framework for a national conversation. Workplace Flexibility 2010, Georgetown Law. Retrieved from http://workplaceflexibility2010.org/images/uploads/whatsnew/ Flexible%20Workplace%20Solutions%20for%20Low-Wage%20 Hourly%20Workers.pdf

ABOUT THE AUTHOR

Ruth Weirich has been a management professional in the publishing industry for 30 years. She has experience in leadership, marketing, training, sales budgets, and financials. She received her MBA from Colorado State and her BA in Business Administration from Goshen College. With a love of maximizing an organization's operating performance and achieving its financial goals, Ruth has held responsibilities ranging from communicating with all stakeholders to preparing operating budgets to overseeing a strategic plan. Ruth is an active listener, a critical thinker, and has quick judgment and decision making skills.

Weirich recently was president of aha! Process. Working for a small company allowed her to have a hands-on experience with all the strategic projects the organization developed. Weirich presents the Workplace Stability training for aha! Process and also consults with executives who are working to stabilize the business and the workforce.

Additional Resources from aha! Process

Workplace Stability Training Supplement

The purpose of this training supplement is to accompany the Workplace Stability workshop (one book for each participant), a training that provides employers and managers tools that address the issues of workplace instability. You'll learn to:

- Recognize the range of factors that create instability for employees
- See how instability, employee performance, and profitability are related
- Identify the most effective techniques and tactics for increasing workplace stability
- Create an action plan best suited to your business and its culture and employees
- Network with other business interests to share resources, training, and more

Getting Ahead in the Workplace

Getting Ahead in the Workplace is a workbook of 16 facilitated sessions to help under-resourced people build resources and gain control over their future stories for a better life at home and at work.

Participants create their own success by investigating:

- The realities of conditions at home/work/ community and how they impact stability
- The "hidden rules" and special language of getting ahead in the workplace
- How to build resources and relationships that open doors and help keep them open
- Practical skills for dealing with change and creating stability at work and at home
- The power of intentionally creating and following a new future story plan

Additional Resources from aha! Process

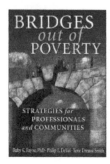

Bridges Out of Poverty

If you didn't grow up in poverty, you may be unaware of the "hidden rules" that govern many aspects of life for the poor. People in poverty are often in survival mode, and support systems taken for granted in middle class and wealth are largely nonexistent. If your business, agency, or organization works with people from poverty, a deeper understanding of their challenges—and strengths—helps you partner with them to create opportunities for success.

Bridges Out of Poverty is a uniquely powerful tool designed for social, health, and legal services professionals. Based in part on Dr. Ruby K. Payne's myth-shattering *A Framework for Understanding Poverty, Bridges* reaches out to millions of service providers and businesses whose daily work connects them with people in poverty. You'll find case studies, detailed analysis, helpful charts and exercises, and specific solutions you and your organization can implement right now to:

- Redesign programs to better serve the people you work with
- Build skill sets for management to help guide employees
- Upgrade training for front-line staff like receptionists, caseworkers, and managers
- Improve treatment outcomes in healthcare and behavioral healthcare
- Increase the likelihood of moving from welfare to work

Hidden Rules of Class at Work

Written for people who supervise others, this book looks at how issues of class determine one's ability to survive in the workplace and offers tools necessary to move to a different level of the organization if one so desires.

Join us on Facebook
www.facebook.com/rubypayne
www.facebook.com/ahaprocess

Twitter
www.twitter.com/ahaprocess
#PovertyChat
#BridgesOutofPoverty

Pinterest
www.pinterest.com/ahaprocess

Subscribe to our YouTube channel
www.youtube.com/ahaprocess

Respond to our blog
www.ahaprocess.com/blog

Download free resources
www.ahaprocess.com